Trapped Emotions

Trapped Emotions

How Are They Affecting Your Life?

Oliver JR Cooper

Also By Oliver JR Cooper

A Dialogue With The Heart – Part One: A Collection Of Poems And Dialogues From The Heart

Note to Readers

That which is contained within this book is based upon my own experiences, research and views up until the point of publication. It is not to be taken as the truth or the only way. And it is not intended to diagnose or cure any disease.

This book is dedicated to Jenny Jones for her support and understanding. Without this, I might not have written this book or been around to write it.

Trapped Emotions – How Are They Affecting Your Life

Edited by - Maddie Northern

ISBN-13: 978-1499208566
ISBN-10: 1499208561

For information, please contact:

www.oliverjrcooper.co.uk

Contents

Introduction...1

Chapter 1: Trapped Emotions 5

Chapter 2: Abandonment..11

Chapter 3: Anger 15

Chapter 4: Anxiety 21

Chapter 5: Attachment...25

Chapter 6: Attraction...31

Chapter 7: Back Pain...37

Chapter 8: Being Present...41

Chapter 9: Beliefs 45

Chapter 10: Body Language 51

Chapter 11: Breakups..55

Chapter 12: Compulsive Behaviour............................61

Chapter 13: Control 65

Chapter 14: Dependency 69

Chapter 15: Depression 75

Chapter 16: Emotional Body 81

Chapter 17: Emotionally Dependent 87

Chapter 18: Emotionally Disconnected 93

Chapter 19: Emotional Instability 99

Chapter 20: Emotional Regulation 105

Chapter 21: Emotionally Stuck................................111

Chapter 22: Empathy...117

Chapter 23: Energy..123

Chapter 24: False Self 127

Chapter 25: Feeling Good....................................131

Chapter 26: Feeling Safe 137

Chapter 27: Forgiveness.....................................143

Chapter 28: Grief 147

Chapter 29: Illness...151

Chapter 30: Inner Child.....................................157

Chapter 31: Inner Conflict 161

Chapter 32: Intimacy..167

Chapter 33: Jealousy 173

Chapter 34: Letting Go......................................179

Chapter 35: Loss 183

Chapter 36: Manifestation...................................187

Chapter 37: Neediness 193

Chapter 38: Negative People 197

Chapter 39: Negative Thoughts...............................201

Chapter 40: Painful Memories................................205

Chapter 41: Physical Pain...................................209

Chapter 42: Rage 213

Chapter 43: Reactive Behaviour 219

Chapter 44: Rejection 225

Chapter 45: Regression...229

Chapter 46: Regret 233

Chapter 47: Relationships.....................................237

Chapter 48: Self-control..243

Chapter 49: Self-harm...247

Chapter 50: Sensitive..251

Chapter 51: Shame..255

Chapter 52: Suicidal 259

Chapter 53: Ungrounded 265

Chapter 54: Victim Mentality 269

Chapter 55: Releasing Your Trapped Emotions.......275

My Story 281

Acknowledgments...287

About The Author 289

Introduction

After having written about trapped emotions for nearly a year, it occurred to me that it would be a good idea to create a book about them.

I believe that if something can't be explained in a simple and easy-to-understand manner, then it shouldn't be written about in the first place. As Albert Einstein once said: "if you can't explain it simply, you don't understand it well enough."

In today's world, there is so much going on; people are under more and more pressure than ever before. And this has meant that there is an increasing need for everything to be simpler and easier to understand.

And this inspired me to set this book out in a way that is easy to access. You don't need to read the whole book in order to learn about a certain emotional area.

It is possible for you to read a certain area without needing to read another part to gain clarity and completion, in regards to what you have just read.

The mind has questions, and so as soon as you have a question about a certain emotion or emotional experience, you can locate the right page and give your mind some food for thought.

This book can be read from page to page, but it doesn't have to be. Nothing will be lost if you read each part at random.

While I have given answers to questions in this book and shared my current views, it is always my intention to be a catalyst to others and not to take away their ability to think for themselves.

We are all on our own personal journey and what works for one person might not work for another. This doesn't necessarily mean that one person is right and the other is wrong; it just means we are all unique human beings.

And this needs to be accepted and embraced, not rejected or dismissed.

My intention for this book is that it will not only enable you to gain a better understanding of what can happen when you have trapped emotions in your body, but also a greater understanding of emotions in general.

And if I am able to assist you in doing that or just make you think differently when it comes to emotions, this book will have served its purpose.

Trapped Emotions – How Are They Affecting Your life?

Chapter 1

Trapped Emotions

Although emotions need to flow and to be expressed during moments when it is appropriate, they are often inhibited and denied the chance to be expressed. Now, there will always be times in one's life when it is not appropriate to express them and yet when one is in a different environment, it will be important that they are released and the emotional flow can return.

However, while the above is the ideal, it doesn't always take place. And as a result of this, emotions will start to build up in one's body. One may not feel that it is safe to express their emotions as an adult and this could have been an outlook that they have had since they were a child.

And so as they have never been allowed to be expressed and released, they had nowhere else to go. One could now have a body that is completely filled with emotions.

Adult Life

As an adult there are all kinds of emotionally charged and traumatic situations that one could have been through. This could relate to the loss of a: family member, friend, lover, or a pet, for instance. Or perhaps it was another kind of loss that related to: a job, business project, or the ending of a relationship.

And while any of these can create extreme pain and suffering, it doesn't mean that this pain and suffering will be dealt with in a healthy way. One could have avoided the emotional experience that they had and the body then had to pay the price.

When this happens, one can forget how they felt (that's if they even knew) and completely lose touch with their emotions. So the mind can then come to conclude that they no longer exist and naively believe that that's the end of it.

Childhood

So even though one's adult years do play a big part in whether or not emotions become trapped in one's body, there is also another time that can be even more important. These are the childhood years and this is a time when one is more dependent on others.

This means that the type of caregivers one had and the other people that were around during this time will typically define whether one felt safe to express one's emotions or not.

Type Of Care

How aware one's caregivers were will often define the type of care received. If one was brought up by a caregiver who was primarily empathic, emotionally available, and in tune, then there would have been less of a need to deny or hide how one felt as a child.

But if one was brought up by caregivers who were unempathic, emotionally unavailable and out of tune; then there is a higher chance that one would have had to hide and deny what was going on emotionally.

Abuse

And in some cases, this could have been due to one being verbally, sexually, emotionally, or physically abused as a child. In each of these cases, one would have had to detach from how they felt (their body) and these feelings and emotions would have ended up staying in their body.

Accumulative Experiences

However, while moments of extreme abuse can be a factor here, it could also have been a consequence of situations that were fairly subtle and pain free. Here, one may have just had situation after situation that was mildly frustrating and disempowering.

And at the time, they didn't cause too much pain, but as these experiences accumulated they became a problem. So at first they could be overlooked and forgotten about, but after a while they completely took over.

As A Baby

While remembering what happened as a child can be tough and sometimes even impossible to do, it can be even harder to get a sense of how one felt as a baby. But even though one may not be able to remember what happened during these very early years, it doesn't mean that they are not important.

As one was so undeveloped at this time, if one was brought up by a caregiver that was emotionally unavailable and out of tune, then one's emotions would have had nowhere to go. The body would then have to absorb these emotions and carry the emotional weight.

Consequences

So above are a few examples of what can lead to trapped emotions. One thing is certain here, and that is that the body is going to feel tight, tense and weighed down. The emotions and feelings that can become trapped in the body include: hopelessness, powerlessness, shame, guilt, anger, rejection, abandonment, betrayal, despair, grief, rage, resentment, fear, anxiety, loss, and panic.

Suicidal feelings can also be trapped in the body, as if no one is around to regulate a child's emotions, it can feel like the end of the world. This is because a child hasn't got the ability to regulate their emotions and so they are overwhelming. Wanting to die is then a normal response to being emotionally abandoned.

And when these emotions and feelings have become trapped in the body, it can lead to all kinds of consequences arising. One's behaviour can be defined by them and the people that one attracts and is attracted to can all be the result of what's going on in the body. Feeling empowered and having self-control can be more or less impossible.

Reactive, violent and abusive behaviour is inevitable if one has a lot of trapped emotions in their body. So is the feeling that one has become emotionally stuck and has not grown up. Having no energy and feeling depressed, addicted, and obsessed can be consequences. Health problems can also arise.

Intimacy And Boundaries

If one has a lot of trapped emotions in their body, it can make it extremely difficult to experience intimacy. And this is because emotions such as rejection, loss, and abandonment can build up in the chest, as well as the fear of getting to close to another in the stomach area.

Having strong and functional boundaries is not going to be possible if one has all these emotions built up. Being enmeshed or dependent on another can seem normal and one can feel that they have no control over their body.

Positive Thinking

This is one reason why positive thinking and changing the mind's thoughts or beliefs doesn't always work. For if one has all these emotions trapped in their body, changing what's going on in the mind is going to do very little. All it may do is create more frustration, anger, and a sense that one has no control over their reality.

It would be like one changing the icing on a cake and expecting the cake itself to change. If the cake is a fruit cake, simply changing the icing won't make it a sponge cake.

Awareness

These emotions that have become trapped in the body will need to be released. When this starts to happen one will be able to experience self-control and perhaps this will be something that has never been experienced before. The need to control others will start to diminish as a result.

Chapter 2

Abandonment

One can have the desire to be in a relationship that is meaningful and fulfilling and yet they might find this hard to achieve. And it could be that they can't seem to attract the right person or that when they are in a relationship with someone who they connect with, it soon ends.

There could be all kinds of reasons as to why this is happening. But if this has become a way of life for this person and something they are accustomed to, then there is likely to be a pattern at work.

At first, this might not be visible and everything could appear to be going on randomly. However, if one was to take a closer look at what is going on and what is not going on in their relationships, they would start to notice certain themes.

This may not be seen straight away and could take a short time to realise. But if one wants to see them and is committed to having exactly what they say they want, then the answers will soon arrive.

The Challenge

Seeing these patterns in one's reality is not the easiest thing to do though and this is partly due to how the mind works. All kinds of illusions can arise and these can end up distracting someone from seeing what is actually occurring.

In the absence of pattern recognition, life is typically seen as random and one is then simply a bystander. And while this can create a momentary sense of relief from having to deal with anything, in the long run one will only end up feeling victimised and that they have no control over their whole life or this area of their life.

Patterns

These patterns then play out without one's awareness and while the people they are attracted to or attract will be different, the same scenarios will be played out. What then happens, and as to how long this takes, may alter, but how one feels will be the same.

Externally there will be certain things that either take place or don't take place, but underneath all of this will be certain feelings. And this could be: abandonment, betrayal, rejection, and loss, for instance.

So even though each relationship will have different experiences, how one ends up feeling is likely to be the same. It is like being in one country and having rain, and going to another to find there is still rain; each place looks different and yet it is still the same story.

Abandonment

When this pattern relates to being abandoned, one might find that they get into relationships and before long they end. This could be one that is going well, and where everything seems to be going to plan, and then out of nowhere, it just finishes.

Or one might not even reach that stage and find that they don't go beyond having a few dates with someone. For example, they could arrange to meet someone for a second date and then this person cancels. This is after a connection has been formed and one has met them. And not only does the date not take place, but they also never hear from the other person again, or if they do, it is in the form of a well-constructed excuse.

Perhaps one doesn't get to the stage of being in a relationship or even going on a date, and the feeling of abandonment is then something that pervades their whole life. Being abandoned could be how they have always felt and so they have no idea that life could be any different.

Two Levels

On one level it is clear that this has no benefit to someone's life and is only creating pain. Intellectually, there is going to be confusion and this could make no sense whosoever. But at a deeper level, this will be what is classed as familiar and therefore safe by one's ego mind.

The problem is that the ego mind probably formed these associations when one was very young, and as time passed, one became cut off from these early experiences. So although one can feel as though the outside world is causing them problems, they are ultimately being victimised by what is going on within them.

Childhood

During one's younger years, one is vulnerable to feelings of abandonment, especially as one's sense of connection comes from being attached to caregivers. At this age, being abandoned could be a matter of life or death. And even if it is not this extreme, it can still end up feeling this way.

So it is vital that one's primary caregiver was attuned to them as a child. This doesn't mean that they had to be perfect, just that they were good enough. Everyone is vulnerable to being abandoned as a child; what complicates this is when one experiences abuse, or some kind of emotional neglect, on a consistent basis, or even just as a one-off experience that was traumatic.

Consequences

When one was abandoned all these years ago, on one side this would have created an emotional experience or many emotional experiences that were painful. And yet on the other side, this experience would have become associated as familiar and therefore safe by the ego mind.

This means that although this experience was not healthy or functional, as far as the ego mind is concerned, it was what was essential to one's survival. And one's whole idea of who they are can be based upon being abandoned, so if this was to change, one might wonder who they are. So all the time these feelings are still trapped in one's body, they will continue to create situations that mirror these early experiences.

These feelings can cause one to push other people away and to behave in ways that will make them leave, so that one can feel abandoned once more. This usually happens unconsciously though, and while it won't get one what they truly want, it is likely to feel comfortable at a deeper level.

Awareness

To move away from this pattern and to no longer feel abandoned as a way of life, or through experiences with others, one will need to release the trapped feelings and emotions that were created in these early experiences. Over the years, additional feelings, thoughts and beliefs will also have accumulated on top of these original feelings and these will go once the original trauma has been dealt with.

Chapter 3

Anger

There are numerous challenges in the world today and some of these challenges are to do with emotions: from depression to suicide and a whole myriad of other things. And emotions cannot simply be ignored or dismissed.

They deserve and need as much attention as one's diet or physical health. However, while diet and exercise are given plenty of exposure in the media and other sources, emotions are generally overlooked.

Emotions can then become something that one: ignores, covers up, runs away from, fights, or gets caught up in. To understand or get in touch with them is then not the focus point; what matters is either pretending they don't exist or ending up being controlled by them.

Two Common Approaches

So this can then lead to one thinking that these are the only options available. One either denies how they feel and uses some kind of repression. Or, they go the other way and have no emotional control.

And in today's society, the first option is typically preferred. These people may be emotionally numb and completely out of touch with how they feel, or just cover up how they feel and pretend that everything is fine.

When it comes to the people who are emotionally out of control and who exercise very little restraint, they are often labelled as being unstable.

The Ideal

So it is fairly clear that neither of these approaches work as a general way of dealing with emotions and feelings. There are always likely to be moments when one denies how they feel, or instantly express how they feel. And that is to be expected; we are only human after all and our self-awareness will desert us from time to time.

Ideally, one would generally be able to just be with their emotions, seek the assistance of another person to help them hold the space when this is not possible, and neither react to nor repress these emotions. This ability would have been developed, in most cases, during one's childhood.

But this is not something that always takes place due to a number of reasons. And this can be the result of having caregivers who were emotionally undeveloped, unavailable, or out of tune with their own emotions.

When this takes place, one can grow up having no understanding of one's emotions and lacking the ability to regulate them. One can develop this ability in later life, but this is often the exception and not the rule. And as their caregivers were not there to regulate how they felt, the emotions and feelings that one felt at that time could have ended up being trapped in one's body.

Consequences

This means that not only can one's body end up carrying a lot of emotions and feelings and therefore being emotionally overloaded, but one also lacks the ability to regulate their emotions.

So it is like having a problem and yet having no way of solving it. It is then not just present-day emotions and feelings that one has to either

16

repress or express without control, but emotions and feelings that are coming up from the body. These could have been there since one was a child, a baby, and even since one was in the womb.

Anger

Anger is one of the common emotional challenges in the world today. Not simply being angry on the odd occasion or when it is required, but feeing overly angry all of the time or when it is not appropriate, for example.

Here once can react with extreme anger when anger is not required or perhaps when expressing anger in a more controlled way might have been better. This person feels extreme anger and is not in control of their anger; they are being controlled by anger.

Popular Solutions

One of the options for someone who has anger problems is to participate in some kind of anger management program. Other options involve certain breathing techniques or changing how one behaves.

These can lead to reduced anger and therefore to responding to situations in a more balanced way. However, what is not always looked at is what is going on at a deeper level. And if one has anger problems, it is often an indicator of inner unrest.

Survival Mechanism

Even though anger is what is creating problems, anger is a secondary occurrence. Anger typically appears when one feels violated and under threat in some way. Through being angry, one feels energised and empowered. Here, one can have the courage to stand their ground and to protect oneself.

A Deeper Level

So for the person who has anger problems, there is likely to be deeper feelings that relate to being violated in some way. These could be a consequence of what has happened in their adult life and could be due to what happened to them during their childhood years.

Just because this happened all those years ago, it doesn't mean that one is no longer affected by it. Feelings that relate to being violated or compromised can remain trapped in the body.

Reality

Due to these feelings being locked inside one's body, one will continue to recreate situations that mirror these early experiences, and to interpret them in ways that do - even if they don't. In the beginning one may have had to constantly be on alert to protect oneself, but while times have changed, the body has not. The body naturally wants to release these feelings in order to heal, but the mind can stop this process from taking place.

And yet if one is out of touch with one's body, the only thing that can register is anger. This is because anger will be on top and what is under the anger can remain hidden for as long as one is stuck in their anger.

Awareness

Anger can be a primary focus and yet anger is simply an effect; it is not a cause. To repress anger is not healthy and when it has built up, expressing it can be unhealthy and, in some instances, dangerous.

By getting in touch with the feelings and emotions that are below the anger and releasing them, one will no longer need to feel as angry. Here, one will be less likely to attract situations where one feels violated, and be less likely to interpret situations in this way.

.

Chapter 4

Anxiety

While anxiety is just one of many emotions that one can experience throughout their life and without too many problems arising, it can also be something that ends up being completely out of control. It is then not just another emotion that one can experience; it is something that can end up defining one's whole life.

Fear, for example, is something that can help or hinder one's life. If fear was removed from someone and they didn't have the ability to feel it, it would be dangerous. One would end up doing things that were far from safe and it probably wouldn't be long until their life would come to an end.

When fear is in its rightful place and not out of control, it will allow one to survive. To instinctively know if something is safe or not is vital for one's survival and not something that should be resisted.

And yet if one was in a constant state of fear, one's life would not be too pleasant either. To be in this position could cause one to be paralysed with fear and their whole life would then come to a standstill. Life would not be something that one embraces and therefore enjoys; it would be something one does their best to avoid.

Out Of Control

So emotions are not negative per se, but they can end up limiting one's quality of life if they end up being out of control. If one is being controlled by their emotions and not experiencing any kind of self-control, then there will be problems.

For one to be in a place of constant happiness and joy would not be likely to be seen as 'negative' at first glance. However, to be this way all the time could cause one to overlook parts of one's life and to even deny certain problems that arise in their life.

Today's Problems

This would not be healthy and yet there are probably more people in the world today that are stuck when it comes to seeing life in a 'negative' way, than people who are stuck when it comes to seeing life in a 'positive' way.

And this is surely why fear and anxiety are issues high on the list of what are described as being mental and emotional problems – rather than suffering from being overly happy or joyful, for instance.

Different Areas

Anxiety is something that one can experience more or less all of the time or it can be something that only appears in certain situations. And even when there is nothing going on externally and one is within an environment that is reasonably safe, for instance, it can still appear.

So this means that while there may be an external reason for its appearance, it can also appear without anyone being around and as a result of what is going on in one's mind and body.

While anxiety can be something one experiences most of the time, it can also appear: just before one has an exam, in social situations, when it comes to talking to the opposite sex, and around authority figures.

Anxiety

When anxiety is experienced, one is going to find that their breathing rate increases. Panic, to one degree or another, will appear, as will the feeling of being overwhelmed. This is not an experience where one is going to feel a sense of control or personal power.

One's mind is going to create all kinds of scenarios, as well as different thoughts. But these thoughts could end up being crowded out by how one feels. So the whole thing could end up being more of an emotional experience than a mental one.

One Approach

Thoughts are often said to create how one feels and based on this outlook, it would then be important for one to change how one thinks. Through doing this, they would be able to either lower their anxiety or stop it from appearing altogether.

And for some people, this will work and that will be the end of it. But what this doesn't look at is what is going on at a deeper level. Because even though so much attention has been placed on our thoughts, when it comes to our level of mental and emotional health, inherently, we are emotional beings.

Survival

How we feel can also define how we think, and our thoughts are not always in control. Anxiety is similar to anger, in that it is there to warn someone that their survival is under threat or that it could be.

So when one is in an environment where this is the case, anxiety is doing what it needs to do and that is to keep one alive. However, when one's survival is not under threat and one still feels anxious, it is clear that something else is going on.

Trapped Emotions

The body can carry trapped emotions and this can be due to one experiencing some kind of trauma. And as the trauma was never processed, it has stayed in their body.

This could have been in their adult life or through what happened during their childhood years. It doesn't have to be something that was extremely traumatising, as it could relate to something that was fairly mild and yet gradually wore one down.

So time has passed and one's mind might have forgotten about what happened, but the body remembers and still carries the emotional pain, therefore continuing to experience life in the same way. These trapped emotions will define how one interprets their reality.

Going Deeper

Under the anxiety could be the feeling of being powerless: that one has no control and even that they are going to die, amongst others (with these feelings being held just above their stomach). For if one didn't feel this way and felt a sense of power, there is not likely to be the need to feel so anxious.

And these feelings can seem completely out of place, based on one's current environment. But if one was to get in touch with what has happened in their past, these feelings could be deemed normal and expected. So as trapped emotions are released from the body, one's anxiety levels are likely to change.

Chapter 5

Attachment

It is often said that attachment creates suffering and this is one of the foundations of Buddhism. And when it comes to attracting something into one's life, attachment is said to be the very thing that will sabotage its arrival.

One only has to look at what one is attached to and what one is not attached to in order to see this dynamic at work. What one is attached to is often what one does not have and what one is not attached to is typically what they do have in their life.

Focus

This shows how important one's focus is in what shows up in their reality and what doesn't. Logically, it seems right that one should place their attention on what they want and keep it there until it shows up.

However, through doing this, what one seeks will continue to allude them. Ideally, the intention is set and then one lets go; while carrying on with what needs to do in each moment of their life.

Obsession

Attachment can easily lead to the ego mind becoming obsessed. For if one is not happy within or is not experiencing a sense of peace; there will be more pressure to get what one is attached to. Through getting this, one will expect to feel better about oneself or feel happier with one's life.

25

So in this case, the more inner turmoil that one has, the more attachment there is likely to be. Through this, one can easily come to the conclusion that peace and happiness are attained through acquiring things.

And when it comes to the modern day world, this is not just a point of view that a small minority have; it has become a 'truth' of the western world. Here, materialism is the new god and will - supposedly - bring an end to people's inner unrest.

The Other Extreme

On the other side of all this is the outlook that one should have no attachments and that materialism should be renounced. And if someone lives in a mountain and has therefore severed all relational ties; then this outlook is probably ideal.

For the individual that is very much part of the world, this way of life is unlikely to work. To be overly attached to things is going to create unnecessary pain, but to have no attachments could lead to one who lacks structure and who doesn't allow themselves to get close to anyone. And to be this way is not going to be practical in today's world.

Trust

To be overly attached to something is often a sign that one doesn't trust that it will show up. Although one may be attached to getting something, if the trust is there, the attachment is minimal.

And when there is so much attachment to something, it can be very difficult to trust and to let go. While it can be normal to blame oneself for getting attached and even try to have no attachment, these approaches rarely work.

Emotional Regulation

When one is experiencing emotional turmoil within, it is often inevitable that external things are going to be sought in order to regulate how one is feeling. And this can relate to all areas of one's life.

Key areas are going to be relationships with: the opposite sex, colleagues, managers, friends, and family members. There is also the potential for strong attachment when it comes to achieving certain milestones in one's life or attaining important things such as a house or a car.

A Closer Look

The painful feelings that can come up in these areas and therefore lead to attachment are: rejection, abandonment, powerlessness, hopelessness, helplessness, shame, guilt, emptiness, worthlessness, fear, and grief, amongst other things.

And once they appear, one desires and wants external things as a way to remove oneself from the inner experience that is taking place. So while attachment can be deemed the problem, if these feelings were not there, then one is unlikely to become so attached in the first place.

Examples

When it comes to relationships and in finding a suitable partner, one can become attached to finding 'the one' or become extremely needy and attached to someone they have just met.

In the work environment, one can complete a task and then spend the rest of the week or month worrying about whether they have done it right. And as they can't let go of the outcome, their whole life becomes consumed by what may or may not happen.

Emotional Power

So while these are simply emotions and feelings, they have incredible power and influence over one's life. How reality is experienced is often the result of how one feels. And to the degree that one is attached to something or not, will also depend on how emotionally settled one is.

But while emotions and feelings can come and go, they can also become stuck and end up being trapped in the body. And one of the consequences of having trapped emotions and feelings is that one can end up becoming inordinately attached to things.

Trapped Emotions

These can relate to emotional experiences that have not been dealt with as an adult and that one had as a child. The mind can be cut off from the body and believe that what happened in the past no longer has any effect on one's life. However, when the mind avoids emotions and feelings, the body can end up paying the price.

The mind can pretend they no longer exist and when this happens, the body will be forced to store them. This can be in one's muscles, organs, bones, and skin.

Modern Day Triggers

Although these emotions and feelings are trapped in the body, they want to be released and let go. In a situation where one becomes overly attached to someone or something, these trapped emotions are coming to the surface and one can then end up believing that the external world is causing them to feel as they do.

But even though external sources can trigger these emotions and feelings, they often have nothing to do with what's going on externally. If one reacts to these feelings, they are also giving away their power to external sources.

Awareness

These feelings and emotions could be seen as parasites, as they can make one want and do things that do not reflect who they are. And as these feelings and emotions are released, one is unlikely to be as attached and what they are attached to can also change.

Because if one no longer feels a sense of shame, rejection, or powerlessness, for example, then their point of focus is inevitably going to change. And by being more at peace within, one can be who they are, instead of trying to be who they are not.

What one actually wants and needs can then show up, with less resistance and struggle.

Chapter 6

Attraction

When it comes to who one is attracted to and attracts, it can appear to be a random process, and that one has no control over who they attract or are attracted to. Certain physical traits are often cited as being the reason why one is or was attracted to someone.

And physical characteristics certainly play an important part in who someone is or is not attracted to. Most people have specific things they like and things that they are not too keen on.

But while physical characteristics are important, they don't always have the biggest influence on who one is attracted to. What often takes precedence over physical appearances is how one feels or doesn't feel at any given moment.

These can be feelings that one is completely aware of or they can be feelings that are just outside of one's conscious awareness. So from time to time they may be known or they could be completely unknown.

The Body

Now, if one is in touch with their feelings and emotions, and therefore their body, they will know how they feel and so they might even see this process taking place. One could feel emotionally centred and together and be attracted to people who are in the same place, so to speak. The connection is then highly visible and there is no mystery as to why one is attracted to such people.

Another example would be when one feels emotionally fragmented and out of balance and finds themselves being attracted to people who are having the same emotional experience. And again, one will soon see the connection and while they may feel frustrated, they will not be surprised as they are in the same emotional place themselves.

The Ideal

To have this connection to one's body and what is going on emotionally is the ideal. One will feel more empowered than if they were disconnected and everything seemed to be happening randomly.

It would be clear that one needs to change how they feel in order to attract people who are emotionally healthy. One would know that they had control and a choice in the matter and were not victims.

The Norm

However, this body and mind connection is not the norm in today's world and this can lead to all kinds of problems. It would then be unclear as to what one was feeling in their body and so seeing the connection between what is going on internally and what is going on externally would not be possible.

Who one is attracted to and attracts would then appear random and as something that one has no control over. The mind would then take over and have the answers to these questions

The Story Maker

While the mind can be disconnected from the body and the real answers, it doesn't mean that it won't come up with all kinds of false reasons as to why certain people are showing up in one's reality. Here, the mind will form interpretations to explain what is going on.

And these interpretations can be the result of what one has learnt through intellectual means.

This could be what they have read, what they have heard through other people, and the interpretations that they have made throughout their life. And while these can seem completely accurate as far as the mind is concerned, in most cases they could be nothing more than fancy ideas. The mind is the observer of life and yet the body is experiencing life in real time.

An Analogy

One can have ideas about what it is like to swim and read numerous books and even watch videos. This will give them an intellectual understanding of swimming. But until they get into the water, it is not a real experience. When they get into the water and swim, it will become real.

In this example, it is clear that one can't understand what it is like to swim unless one goes into the water. And yet when it comes to understanding why we attract the people that we do, it is not always as easy to realise. This is generally due to one being disconnected from one's body and being cut off from the body's wisdom.

Pain

When there is pain in the body and this pain is too hard to handle, it is natural and normal for one to stay in their head and to leave their body. This could be something one does from time to time and during different moments, or it could be something that has become a way of life.

Perhaps one has experienced some kind of trauma as an adult or when they were a child, or it could relate to an accumulation of experiences that gradually wore one down. And one's time as a baby and even in the womb can all have an effect. So it feels safe to live in one's head and too painful to be in one's body.

Trapped Emotions

And when one is disconnected from their body and therefore lives primarily in their head, it will be a mystery as to what is going on in the body. This can mean that feelings and emotions will have become trapped in their body. They can be in one's: skin, bones, muscles, and vital organs.

Consciously one is then oblivious to these emotions and feelings, but that doesn't mean they are not having an effect on one's life. These trapped feelings and emotions will create a resonance and the people who come into their life will mirror this resonance.

It is then not just about the individual emotions and feelings, it is also about the general feelings that they create. This can include feeling: powerless, worthless, unlovable, empty, desperate, hopeless, helpless, rejected, abandoned, violated, betrayed, and fearful.

Familiarity

The ego mind will want to hold onto these feelings as they will be interpreted as familiar and therefore safe. So while they may not cause one to attract the kind of people that one wants, they will feel comfortable to the ego mind. To let go and to embrace other people would be classed as death.

Awareness

The emotions and feelings need to be released from the body and as they are released, one can return to their natural state of inner harmony. And as this takes place, who one is attracted to and attracts will gradually begin to change.

Chapter 7

Back Pain

There is the potential for one to experience pain in all areas of their body. These can relate to one having a headache, stomach problems, tension in their shoulders and/or their lower back, for instance.

It is highly likely one has experienced at least one of the above this year, let alone throughout one's whole life. For some people, they could be regular experiences and what has become part of everyday life.

To live this way from time to time may not cause too many problems, but to constantly be under pressure in all or even one of these areas, is going to affect one's wellbeing. The pain doesn't even need to be too extreme, because if it is there on a fairly consistent basis, it is going to wear one down.

Build Up

There is also the potential for this pain to start off as irritating and annoying and then for it to build up. So as time passes, one could end up being overwhelmed and taken over by it. And other consequences could then appear and cause even further pain.

This process could be very linear and the pain could get worse as the minutes, hours, and days go by. Or it could just flare up and then return to how it was before. Other factors can also make a big difference in how this pain fluctuates.

Other Factors

The common factors relate to: what one has or hasn't been doing physically, what they have or haven't eaten, and how stressed they are. Genetics are also likely to be a contributing factor.

So through taking into account factors such as the ones above, one could: change their diet, exercise more, and try to keep stress levels to a minimum. This approach will be enough for some people or may, at the very least, take away some of the pain.

A Closer Look

It will be pretty normal, then, for one to be asked about what they have been eating, if they have been doing any exercise, and even about their state of mind. But what is not as likely to take place is for someone to be asked about their emotional state.

If they were around a doctor or a similar figure that was emotionally aware, then this could take place. And yet this is more of an exception than a rule in the western world and countries influenced by the western world.

The Connection

So when one experiences physical pain, it is often seen as merely the body playing up in some way; one has no control over what is going on 'down there'. To be human means that one is, fundamentally, an emotional being.

Emotions need to be faced and released, and therefore to flow much like a river. If this can't take place as they arise, then this needs take place soon after they have appeared. When they are not processed in some way, they will not simply disappear.

They can end up being stuck in ones vital organs and muscles. And as they are trapped in one's body, consequences will arise sooner or later.

Cut Off

However, even though these emotions have remained in one's body, it doesn't mean that one is aware of it. One can end up living on their head and have no awareness as to what is going on inside their body.

Emotions are generally overlooked, and as repression is very common in today's world, not only is one unlikely to have a healthy relationship with their emotions, but they could also have an emotional build-up within them.

This build-up can be the result of what has happened throughout adult life, as well as what has happened during the childhood years. Years end up passing and the mind can forget all about what happened, and yet the body is only too aware of what took place.

Back Pain

And these trapped emotions can cause one to experience physical pain in their back, as well as other areas of the body. But of course this is not black and white, as back pain can be due to a physical strain, an accident, or even how someone has been sleeping, for example.

The lower part of the body relates to survival: for instance, having enough money, food, and having the feeling of being supported by others. Within the physical pain in these areas the following feelings can be held: abandonment, hopelessness, powerlessness, and death.

These feelings may sound rather extreme and yet they often have their roots in what took place as a baby or child. How supported one feels as an adult often depends on the kind of nurturing they received growing up.

Support

As soon as one is born, one is dependent on the support of caregivers. If they are generally around to take care of one's wants and needs, then one is likely to grow up feeling supported.

But if this support was not consistent or was, in some cases, nonexistent, then one would have had the odd moment or many moments where they felt: abandoned, hopeless, powerless, that they were going to die. The mind would have created beliefs and thoughts and then these would have been taken as truths about life.

To be left would mean that these feelings would not have been regulated by anyone and would have had to have been pushed out of one's awareness.

Awareness

And as these feelings remained in one's body and the mind held onto the beliefs and thoughts, one would have had no choice than to recreate the same reality all over again as an adult. The environment might be different, but the experience will be the same and the same patterns will appear.

To see that these beliefs are not the truth will be one thing; the next stage will be to release these trapped feelings and emotions.

Chapter 8

Being Present

Ever since Eckhart Tolle's book, *The Power Of Now*, came out, being present has consumed the self help industry. Even people who were not into self-development came across this book.

Interpretation

And whether a teacher is speaking about being present or whether they are talking about how to make a cake, there is always going to be a variation in people's interpretations of what something means.

These interpretations can be accurate and match up to what is being communicated or they can be completely inaccurate and have nothing to do with what is being communicated. The present moment is all there is and when one is not present then they are out of touch with the only moment that matters.

So although it is clear that being present is the ideal, it is not always easy to be present. At times, it can seem impossible and nothing more than a good idea.

And as it can be so difficult, it can result in one denying how they really feel or what they are thinking, and all because they want to be present.

Repression

Being present then becomes a new name for denial and repressing how one truly feels. At first, this may seem like a great idea and one that may work for a short period of time.

Like a new toy that a child receives from its caregivers, in the beginning, the toy consumes the child's attention and shortly after, it is thrown away just like the rest of its toys. The child's short attention span is still there and is not going anywhere - no matter how many toys are given.

The same process applies to emotions, feelings, and thoughts. If they are denied and covered up, it is unlikely to lead to one being present. These issues will come back, but when they do, they may be even stronger.

Thoughts

The primary focus when it comes to self-development and change is often one's thoughts. These are often said to be the biggest challenge in one being present. So when the mind settles down, one can then experience a greater sense of peace and harmony within.

So from this point of view, the mind is the only thing that matters and the body is therefore irrelevant. But if one was to become aware of one's thoughts, they would often see that they are nothing more than a consequence of how they are feeling in their body.

The Body

Feelings and emotions are within the body and based on these, the mind responds accordingly. When these are unpleasant feelings and emotions, it is normal for the mind to become obsessed and to think endlessly about certain things. And these thoughts can be positive or negative.

This is a defence mechanism that the mind uses to regulate pain and to ensure its own survival. For if there was too much pain it could be overwhelming and lead to death.

So the minds thoughts are a way to calm everything down and to avoid the pain that is coming up from the body.

The Present Moment

It may sound like the right thing to do to let go of one's thoughts, but these thoughts are often only appearing as a result of what is going on inside the body. When the body is at a place of peace, the mind is likely to follow suit.

And the pain that can build up inside the body can cause someone to reject their body and to live in their head. This is done because it feels safer than living in a body that is full of pain.

A lot of focus has been placed on thoughts over the years, and this has resulted in the power of the body being rejected. And yet the body is where one's power really lies and where the answers are found.

Trapped Emotions

If one lives in their head due to what has built up in their body, there is likely to be many trapped emotions and feelings. When the body is at peace, the mind can relax. But when the body is in pain, the mind will end up thinking excessively.

These can be emotions and feelings that have become trapped as a result of what has happened to someone as an adult and what took place during their childhood years.

This can include the following feelings and emotions: rejection, abandonment, betrayal, grief, fear, rage, resentment, anger, helplessness, hopelessness, shame, guilt, and fear.

And just because they are trapped in the body, it doesn't mean that they are not having an effect on one's life. They are constantly seeking to be heard in one way or another.

Letting Go

When one is present and in the moment, one is likely to be free of fear and other restrictive emotions. But if these feelings and emotions are trapped in the body, it is going to be practically impossible to be present.

And this is why it is important to let go of what has built up in the body. When this happens, being present will not be a struggle or something that involves force. It will be something that naturally takes place and all because there is peace within the body.

Awareness

In many ways, the mind is simply a reflection of what is going on in the body. So getting in touch with one's feelings and emotions and releasing them is very important.

Chapter 9

Beliefs

If someone is behaving in a certain way or not attracting what they want into their life, it is often said to be a result of what their beliefs are. And so one then needs to change what they believe, in order to act differently and to attract what they want into their reality.

A large part of the self-development industry is focused on beliefs and there have been many techniques and methods created to change beliefs. Some of these approaches have been around for many, many years and others are fairly recent inventions, or what could be described as a blend of previous ways.

The Mind

This means that one's primary focus is on what is going on in the mind and not what is taking place within one's body. The mind is where beliefs are found and where thoughts, ideas, assumptions, expectations, and associations are formed.

So the mind is not directly involved with the here and now; if anything, it supplies feedback to what is taking place. For when one is in the moment, there is neither feedback nor ideas about reality. One is consumed by the moment and has no need to formulate any ideas.

An Analogy

In recent years, cameras have become an essential part of most people's lives. And technology has continued to advance so that they are not only getting smaller, but also cheaper.

45

This has opened the use of cameras up to more people, and, when also considering the addition of cameras to phones, it becomes clear that pictures can be taken during any moment that one has the urge to take them. However, photos are not life itself; they are copies of life.

And this reflects the difference between the mind and the body. The body is the experience, the mind is the picture. In the former, there is complete engagement with reality, whereas the other is a by-product or consequence of it.

The Body

To be in the body, is to be at one with life and everything that is taking place in this moment. There is no past or future in the body; all there is, is now. So in the body's natural state, there is no holding on. The mind, on the other hand, holds on, as holding on is seen as essential to one's survival.

What one is holding onto is what is familiar, and what is familiar is what is safe. So from this point of view, to let go would mean death. And taking pictures, as mentioned in the example above, is a way for the mind to hold onto an experience.

The body has no need to believe or disbelieve anything. But the mind is constantly forming interpretations based on what it experiences and what is doesn't experience. However, the mind can stop the body from expressing certain feelings and emotions.

Feelings

So whereas the mind responds to reality in one way, the body responds to it in another way. And this is through: feelings, emotions and sensations. These are one's first point of experience. Before one

46

even thinks, believes, or forms ideas about life, feelings will at first appear. And this is true when one is a baby and also when one is an adult.

And yet, if one is cut off from their body and lives in their head, it can seem as though what is going on in their mind is causing what is going on in their body. The following quote really encapsulates this: "although many of us may think of ourselves as thinking creatures that feel, biologically we are feeling creatures that think" - Jill Bolte Taylor.

The Truth

The mind will interpret how one feels within one's body to mean certain things. And to the mind, these interpretations will be taken as the truth about reality, oneself, and others.

To the mind, there is no middle ground or grey area. So these feelings will be taken as absolute truths, even though they are simply ideas about life - ideas that can be proven accurate or inaccurate, depending on what one focuses on.

Beliefs

So something can happen in one's life and this will cause their body to create certain feelings and emotions; the mind will then take these to mean something. And these meanings will become beliefs. This could relate to what has happened during one's adult years and go back to when one was a child, with these moments ranging from being mildly or extremely traumatic.

If one felt safe enough to express how they felt or if there was a caregiver around to soothe and mirror them, in the case of a child, there might be no reason for beliefs to be formed. But if these feelings and emotions are denied and covered up, then beliefs will inevitably form.

These beliefs can cover everything from: whether people can be trusted, if one is likeable or not, if one deserves to have money, if the world is a safe place, healthy relationships, and numerous others. There are ultimately no limits to what the mind can believe or disbelieve; there are infinite potentials. Sometimes these beliefs can aid one's life, and at others times they can limit it and even destroy it.

Reality

Although beliefs are just that - beliefs - they will come to define what one experiences and does not experience. They will become the fabric of one's personal reality, and whatever doesn't correspond with these beliefs in one's mind will be filtered out.

This is because the mind is constantly looking for that which it believes to be true. So if something is not seen as the truth, one is unlikely to experience it in their reality. It will always seem out of their grasp, and one could end up seeing themselves as unlucky, unfortunate, or even victimised.

Trapped Feelings

One way would be to change these beliefs and that may work for some people. Another way would be to release the trapped feelings and emotions in one's body. As this takes place, one's reality will change and the mind will have no choice but to change the beliefs that it has created.

What one attracts and doesn't attract will change, and this includes people, circumstances, and areas of materialism. The mind will have a different reality to observe and no reason to believe the same things.

Self-fulfilling Prophecy

In some cases, even if these beliefs were changed, the same reality would still be created. And this is because the feelings that are creating one's reality are still there and have not been faced and released.

So one would create the same reality and yet more beliefs would be formed and then added to the ones that already exist. And the more beliefs that one picks up, the harder it will be to see otherwise and the more one is likely to attract what corresponds to the beliefs.

One could end up being trapped in a cycle that doesn't seem to end. A bit like cutting off a weed and finding that, before long, it grows back. To stop this process, one needs to go to the root of the weed. And in this case, the root relates to the trapped feelings in one's body.

Awareness

If one is stuck in their head, it might be necessary to deal with these beliefs for a while, at least until one can become the observer of their mind. Once one has developed the ability to observe their mind and does not get caught up by it in most cases, then they will be able to get into their body.

Chapter 10

Body Language

When it comes to the words that someone uses, there is the potential for one to cover up what is really going on. One can say what they think they should be saying or what sounds right. And while another person can take this as the truth, it could be a half-truth or even a complete fabrication.

This is why it is important for one to look at what else a person is communicating. And one of the biggest sources of information lies in what their body is giving off. While this can be manipulated just as words can be, to cover up what is taking place internally, it is much harder to do.

Unconscious Communication

While the mind can be monitored and kept under control, the body is a lot harder to control and this is because it has a mind of its own. Another name for the body is the unconscious mind and body language often goes on unconsciously.

People generally read body language unconsciously as well, meaning that their mind may have one idea about someone and their body or intuition could have something else to tell them.

Vital

So as body language plays a massive role in how one comes across, it is going to be a vital element in understanding what another person is saying. It is also going to be important for one to be aware of what their body language is, in order to come across as they want to and to make the right impression.

51

Focus

The next logical step would then be for one to place their attention on the body: to become aware of what their body is doing during certain situations, and how different environments affect them.

As there are plenty of books available on this subject, it is not going to take too much effort to understand body language. Although one may have been unaware of how their body has been reacting throughout their life, it is not as if one is trying to understand a foreign language.

So within a short amount of time, big improvements can be made. At first it may seem strange, but as time goes by, it will become a lot easier and, finally, it will become natural and something one does not even need to think about.

Mind Over Body

This is a clear example of the mind controlling the body. If the body is causing one to come across as closed off, submissive, nervous, or shy, then this will be seen as the right thing to do.

What it can also lead to is one overlooking the reasons as to why their body is responding as it does. These reactions could be seen as insignificant - that perhaps one just needs to force their body to change.

Results

To simply change one's body language is going to cause one to come across differently; that can't be denied. As a result of this, other people are generally going to respond to this person differently.

For some people this will be enough and before long it will feel congruent. And yet for others, changing what their body does will not make much of a difference.

For example, some people may find that their whole life has been transformed, as well as their relationships. Other people may find that their life hasn't really changed and that how they truly feel is just being covered up and repressed. So on the outside they might look the part and yet, on the inside, they could feel like a fraud.

The Solution

Through taking on another person's advice or through one's own conclusions, one could simply carry on with what they are doing with the belief that they will feel different through repetition and that others will soon recognise this difference.

Another option would be for one to get in touch with their body and to see why it reacts as it does. One is likely to see that there are certain patterns in regards to how their body responds around people.

Examples

So one could find that they close up when around the opposite sex, or when anyone gets too close to them. Being around big groups of people or when one is in public could also have the same effect.

Trapped Emotions

The reasons one's body is responding in these ways is not necessarily because of what is taking place externally, but because of how one's mind is interpreting what is taking place. And what is taking place externally, is then triggering certain emotions internally.

So through one feeling as they do, one's body will then do what feels comfortable. If one feels vulnerable or fearful, then they are naturally going to cross their arms, for instance. These emotions could have been trapped in their body for many years.

And what these present day circumstances are doing is reminding them of what happened all those years ago. Their mind may have forgotten all about what happened, but their body remembers.

Postures

One could find that their head is generally tipped forward or that their shoulders are rounded. Now, one approach would be to lift their head and to push their shoulders back. But what this doesn't do is look at why their body is doing this.

And the reason they do this could be to protect their heart. Not only does the heart have a physical use, it is also where feelings of grief, sadness, loss, rejection and abandonment are held. So if one were to be carrying trapped emotions there, then to have a closed posture would be normal and feel 'comfortable'.

Awareness

When one does have trapped emotions in their body, these emotions will need to be released. As this happens, one will find that their body language changes naturally.

Chapter 11

Breakups

One may experience the end of a relationship without experiencing too much pain or could instead experience immense pain and suffering when a relationship comes to an end. It could then be hard to comprehend what is taking place and why this person is having this effect.

The relationship doesn't even need to be one that was fulfilling; it could have been average or even abusive, for instance. It also doesn't need to be one that lasts that long, as it could last for only a short period of time and still result in pain being created.

The Common Reasons

There has been a greater focus on the brain in recent times and on the chemicals that the brain emits. Each of these chemicals has a certain purpose and an effect on how one feels.

The chemicals that are often mentioned in relationships are oxytocin and dopamine. Oxytocin is typically classed as the trust or love chemical. Dopamine is to do with feeling happy.

When a relationship comes to an end these are naturally going to subside and are no longer going to be created in such high amounts. As what one was experiencing is no longer there, it is inevitably going to lead to pain.

Withdrawal

Just as a drug addict would feel tense, uptight, or even suicidal if they didn't get their regular dose, someone whose relationship has ended can feel the same way. But while the drug addict would be missing something that often comes in the shape of a tablet or some kind of powder, in this case what is missing is a person.

The Good Times

A breakup will also mean that all of the good times and special moments that were shared will have come to an end. The physical touching, the sharing, and the support will no longer be there.

One may even have planned their life around this person and this can range from going on a trip together, to having children, and getting married. These plans could be relatively small or monumental and define one's whole life.

Loss

What is clear is that the stakes can be extremely high and there is so much that one can lose through a relationship coming to an end. It can feel as though one's life has come to an end and that life no longer has any meaning.

So the ending of a relationship is not something that should be taken lightly or dismissed as something one should simply get over and move on from. It is a very delicate area and one that needs to be treated with compassion, care, and patience.

The Ego Mind

Another important factor in why relationships can cause so much pain when over is in how the ego mind functions. When a relationship begins and as it progresses, it will feel good and be pleasurable. Although these are wonderful experiences, they are nothing like the experience of a relationship ending.

To gain something is all well and good, and yet to lose something will generally leave a bigger mark. One may gain something without taking much notice, while when something is lost, one cannot help but notice.

The ego mind typically forms associations of familiarity around what one has regularly come to experience and this is what will be classed as safe. This process can take place around experiences that are functional and dysfunctional.

If one were to make a change from something that was unhealthy in their life to something that is healthy, it can be interpreted as death by the mind. This is because it is not familiar and is therefore seen as unsafe.

Ultimately, any kind of change will be seen in the same way. And when a relationship ends, one is going from what was familiar to what is unfamiliar. Even though at one point (in the beginning) the relationship was unfamiliar, it gradually became known as familiar to the mind. So this will be experienced as death and this is another reason why the end of a relationship can hurt so much.

The Past Returns

When one is in a relationship it can be going along nicely and without too much pain, but when it ends, extreme pain can be experienced. And with the reasons above aside, this can be due to one's unprocessed history coming to the surface.

The emotions and feelings that one has carried since childhood, and that relate to one's caregivers, will appear once more. Relationships are often described as vehicles that have the potential to lead one into wholeness.

These feelings can include the following: grief, sadness, hopelessness, helpless, powerlessness, loss, anger, rage, betrayal, rejection, and abandonment. One can even have suicidal feelings and end up feeling depressed.

Although time has passed and one has physically grown up, these emotions and feelings will have remained trapped in the body, and will be triggered by a relationship ending.

Projection

However, one can easily come to conclude that these feelings and emotions are simply the result of the relationship ending. And while some of them can be, they could also have nothing to do with the current relationship.

Here it can be normal for one to project these feelings onto the other person and to believe that they are a reflection of how the relationship was. However, in reality, it is the result of the past being projected onto the present and may have very little to do with how the relationship was or who the other person is.

Awareness

There are many factors as to why the end of a relationship can hurt so much, and getting over this pain is unlikely to be something that happens overnight. But while a lot of pain can be experienced, it can also lead to incredible personal growth and to a greater wholeness.

The emotions and feelings that have built up will need to be released, and it will be important that one reaches out for support from family and friends.

There may be a tendency to find another lover to regulate this pain and yet this can often lead to more problems down the line and stop one from grieving. So in the short term it may feel like a good idea, but in the long term it could just result in more problems.

Chapter 12

Compulsive Behaviour

One of the biggest challenges when it comes to acting in ways that are healthy and functional is something known as compulsive behaviour. This is something that has received widespread publicity in recent years.

When someone behaves in ways that are compulsive, it means that they are not acting in a conscious manner. Here, they feel as though they have no control over what they do or don't do.

It is as if they are possessed by some kind of force and are quite simply powerless to change what is taking place. There are going to be some instances where this kind of behaviour is looked upon with acceptance and other times when it is seen as dysfunctional and unhealthy.

Examples

If one was to compulsively go to the gym or to engage in some kind of exercise, in the short term, it could be seen as productive. And yet if this went on for too long or started to have a negative impact on other areas of one's life, it would be dysfunctional and unhealthy.

When one leaves their house and locks their door, it would be normal to check it at least once on the odd occasion when doubts arise as to whether they have actually locked it or not. But if one was to go back to the door every time that they lock it and check the door five times for example, it is a sign that something is not right.

Another common occurrence is around cleaning one's hands and cleanliness in general. To make sure that one is clean and well-kept can be a reflection of how much they respect and value themselves. However, if this is taken to the extreme and one is constantly washing their hands, then something is out of balance within.

Emotional Regulation

While these behaviours are not always functional and healthy, they enable one to feel more relaxed and at ease, at least for a short time. So one can feel a sense of anxiety, fear, shame, or guilt, and behaving in these ways allows one to regulate their emotions.

As these behaviours repress the emotions and don't deal with them, it means that these behaviours or rituals have to be performed constantly. This is why they become compulsive, for if one did something only once, it would not be enough.

Control

What these compulsive behaviours allow is for the ego mind to feel a sense of control. Although one is clearly out of control, the mind is in control of being out of control. The ego operates through control; to be out of control would be interpreted as death to the mind.

This is because when something is familiar to the mind, it becomes what is classed as safe, so when something is out of control or unfamiliar, it will cause one to feel unsafe. Whether it is functional or healthy is irrelevant. So in this instance, one's mind has learnt to become comfortable through acting in ways that are compulsive. If one didn't act in these ways, pain would be experienced and it wouldn't feel safe.

The ego mind has numerous defence mechanisms to avoid the pain that is coming up from the body. If this pain is not dealt with by the mind's defence mechanisms, it would lead to one being overwhelmed by emotions and feelings.

Conflict

But even though the mind does have these ways of dealing with pain, they are not long-term solutions and are only short-term solutions at best. And when this emotional pain is not dealt with, it will cause one to act in ways that one has no control over.

A body that is full of trapped emotions and feelings is going to be far too much for the mind to handle - rather like trying to put a forest fire out with a watering can. The thoughts that one has around compulsive behaviour are a result of the mind interpreting how one feels - 'my body feels this way, so therefore I think this way'.

The Typical Approaches

One could try to change one's behaviour, and this is going to be a struggle all the time they feel as they do. To behave in another way will only cover up these feelings and cause one to become even more disconnected from them.

Changing one's thoughts might settle the mind down and have a small impact on one's behaviour. However, the feelings in the body are still there and so it will be a battle between body and mind.

Trapped Emotions

If the trapped feelings and emotions were not in the body, the mind would not have to interpret them and create negative thoughts as a consequence. If the body were at peace, then there would be no need to act in dysfunctional ways to regulate how one felt.

These trapped emotions can be the result of what has happened during one's adult years and go back to when one was a child and even a baby. When one doesn't feel that it is safe to express their feelings and emotions (perhaps because the emotional support is not there), they can up being stored in the body. This can be in one's: skin, bones, muscles, and organs.

Awareness

While these feelings and emotions that are trapped in the body can end up controlling how one behaves, they do not belong there. So it can feel as though one is being controlled by something and that they have no control.

As these trapped emotions are released, one's mind and body can work together instead of fighting each other. And one can choose how one behaves, as opposed to feeling that it is out of their control.

Chapter 13

Control

What is common in today's world and throughout history is the idea of control, but in most cases this is not self control, it is the control of others. And this can be seen at all levels of the modern day world, from the personal relationships that people have, to the authority figures of the world.

To have a certain amount of control is healthy and not dysfunctional or unhealthy per se. It is when this natural need is taken to the extreme that problems can arise. This could relate to someone who tries or does control their spouse, family, friends, or children, but could also relate to authority figures that have greater control due to their position, and who desire to control hundreds or even millions of people.

It is clear that there are many areas of control and that it can take place inside people's houses as well as society and the world at large. In many ways it has become normal and what people expect to experience in life.

Feelings

It is often said that everything we do is for a feeling. So by attaining something, one can feel different, either momentarily or for a while. Once this feeling has gone, one may be able to do the same thing all over again.

This can all depend on how one is trying to feel. For instance, if one feels exhausted and wants to feel relaxed, or feels low on energy and wants to feel more alive, then this is not necessarily going to result in one needing to control another.

65

One can watch a film, have a lay-down to relax, go to the gym, or have a run to gain more energy. But if one feels that they have no control over certain situations or their whole life, then this can lead to a different set of consequences.

Control

Here one can feel the need to control other people and this can be for a short while or can last for quite some time. And one may try to control some people in their life and this could go as far as trying to control everyone.

In most cases, the primary control one has is over themselves and in how they respond to what takes place in their life. So one can act in certain ways and what then happens is often out of their control.

Self-control

To find this, one will need to have a sense of self-control. For if one doesn't have this, there will be a greater need to control what is going on externally. And yet if one has a lot of emotional unrest going on, it can be extremely difficult to have self-control.

While feelings may be simply feelings, and do not reflect reality, they can be incredible powerful and define how one sees themselves, others, and life itself.

Out Of Control

Being out of control within can result in someone wanting to control other people. But although other people can be controlled and these inner feelings can be covered up, they won't simply go away.

One can literally feel powerless within, and this can relate to being emotionally out of control. Here, one could feel powerless as a consequence of feeling rejected, abandoned, hopeless, or cut off, for example. These feelings can be so strong that one can come to conclude that controlling others it the only way to deal with them.

Emotional Build-up

The reason these feelings can be so powerful is due to them building up throughout someone's life. People and certain events may appear to make one feel powerless, but these are often simply triggering the feelings and emotions that have built up.

While these feelings can be from experiences that one has had as an adult, they are often the result of what happened when one was a child.

Childhood

If one had a caregiver that was emotionally available and in tune, it would mean that in most cases one would have had their needs and wants met. During times of emotional unrest they would have been regulated by their caregiver, and so they wouldn't have had to deny how they felt or push it out of their awareness to survive.

However, if their caregiver was emotionally unavailable and out of tune, they would have had their needs and wants ignored in most cases. And when one felt emotionally unstable, their caregiver may have been dismissive or absent in some way. This means that the pain they experienced would have gone into their body, simply because no one was around to regulate their emotions.

There may have been moments of mild to extreme abuse and this would have created pain; there would only have been one place for it to go and that would be into the body.

The Body

So as these emotions and feelings are stored in the body and not processed, they come to define how one feels. One's muscles, bones, skin, and organs will carry the burden. And when these feelings are triggered, self-control can completely disappear.

The mind can think whatever it wants, but the body can overpower the mind. It's the difference between a rain drop and a tidal wave.

Awareness

As these feelings and emotions are released, one will start to experience a better connection with their body and self-control will be a natural consequence. The need to control others will subside, and this is because as one feels a greater sense of personal control, there won't be the need to use others to cover up how they feel.

One will come to know and trust that their needs and wants will be met and fulfilled in most cases.

Chapter 14

Dependency

In the area of self-development and recovery, the term co-dependency has been used for many years. This generally describes someone who is not interdependent or independent; they are completely dependent on others or on certain substances.

This is something that can relate to every need that one can have, from the need to be: emotionally, physically, and financially supported, for example. One's fulfilment is then only possible through relying on someone or something.

One is not operating from a place of trust and personal empowerment and neither does one have healthy boundaries. What is in their place is doubt, disempowerment, and the opposite of boundaries - enmeshment. This person sees another person or thing as being essential to their survival. If the person or thing were to be removed, for a short time or completely, this would be likely to cause withdrawal symptoms.

But while co-dependency is not a term that is familiar to everyone, dependency is something that the majority of people can understand. One might observe it in their own lives or in the lives of people they know or hear about through the media.

Separation

Whether it is about one feeling reliant on a person for emotional support or on a substance in order to handle each day, one is still separate from them. Another person will have their own needs and wants, and one cannot become one with them.

It might be possible for someone to feel emotionally connected and lose themselves in the process, but physically they are still separate human beings and always will be. So for as long as this person stays around they will be fine, but if they are not around, there will be problems.

In the case of one being reliant on a substance, one needs to constantly consume it. There is no other option available. And when this substance is no longer available, all kinds of problems will inevitably arise.

Examples

When someone feels dependent, it will invariably relate to the relationships where they have felt the strongest emotional connection. So this means: family, friends, partner/lovers, and children.

Family

To be dependent on one's family could mean that one feels completely reliant on them for emotional and financial support. This could result in one still living with their caregiver/s or living nearby and not going too far away from them.

It would then include receiving money from them and if they didn't receive this money, it could lead to one having financial problems and being unable to support oneself in life.

Partner/Lovers

In the situation where one is dependent on their partner, it would seem that one's whole life rests upon that person being there for them. And if they were not there, one's life wouldn't be worth living and they wouldn't be able to survive.

Children

Although caregivers are adults and can have children who have grown into adults themselves, they could feel that they are dependent on them. The roles have then reversed.

This can relate to their adult child/children supporting them financially, as well as emotionally. Their purpose in life has remained attached to them and they have not emotionally grown out of this. And without them around, they could feel: empty, powerless, abandoned, and lifeless.

Survival

So while each of these examples covers a different emotional attachment, the same dynamics are taking place. One has come to associate their survival as being attached to another person. They have not realised their own sense of personal power and inner strength.

Boundaries have not formed to allow them to know they are actually separate from the other person, and that the person is separate from them. Emotionally they feel that they are one and the same and that there is no difference between them.

Conflict

While this person may be physically an adult, emotionally they are still seeing the world and behaving as if they were a child or even a baby. And when someone is an adult, they will be expected to behave like one. As a child or a baby, one will feel dependent on others and this is normal.

However, if one is an adult and they still feel like a child or a baby emotionally, acting like an adult is unlikely to happen. So feeling a sense of personal power and having the strength to handle life is going to be a real challenge.

Trapped Emotions

And these trapped feelings and emotions can relate to a child or baby that that was abused and/or emotionally neglected, for instance. Time has passed and one's physical body has grown, but what hasn't changed is how one feels. These feelings can go right back to when one felt: powerless, hopeless, helpless, worthless, empty, suicidal, rejected, and abandoned.

It could be that one has become dependent on someone or some kind of substance, but the reasons are still the same. They are allowing one to regulate their emotional pain. If these people leave or if the substances are not available, these trapped feelings and emotions will arise once more.

Awareness

These trapped feelings and emotions need to be released from the body. Due to them remaining in one's body, one has continued to feel as one did when dependent on one's caregivers.

As these emotions are released, one will be able to embrace their inner power and strength. Boundaries will also form and one will see that there is only so much another person can give, and only so much that one can offer another. Having a sense of self will be possible and one won't need to enmesh with another person in order to have an identity and to feel supported.

Trapped Emotions – How Are They Affecting Your life?

Chapter 15

Depression

In today's world, depression has become a word that carries enormous weight, either for people who have it or for people who hear about it. It could be described as a modern day taboo, with people often wanting to avoid the whole thing altogether.

However, what is clear is that depression is not something that can be ignored. It is a very real challenge in today's world, and just one aspect of what are often described as 'mental health' problems.

This is not something that can be cited as having one cause, as there are often said to be numerous causes. These can be: genetics, diet, repression, chemical imbalance, abuse, illness, the environment, and many other factors.

And as we are all so different, it's not a case of one cause being the same for everyone. So as this is such a complex area and not something that can be put into one box, I will cover one of the above aspects that can cause depression.

Depression

On the Google home page, it is described as the following -
1. Severe despondency and dejection, accompanied by feelings of hopelessness and inadequacy.
2. A condition of mental disturbance, typically with lack of energy and difficulty in maintaining concentration or interest in life.

So here, one feels at a low ebb and is unable to feel any positive emotions. Their energy is gone and the will to live doesn't exist either.

Emotions

While depression is often treated as a taboo, emotions are not too far behind in this respect. They are generally ignored and this is partly due to a lack of understanding in how to deal with them. One is not simply born with emotional intelligence; this is something that has to be learnt.

And when it comes to how one responds to and perceives their emotions, the childhood years are typically the most important time. This time will often define what kind of relationship one will have with their emotions.

This relationship can be just like a relationship that one has with other human beings; it can be positive and empowering, or negative and distempering. So emotions can be seen as problems and as something that one needs to avoid or as feedback and as something that one needs to listen to.

The Education System

One of the reasons that this time is so important is that one doesn't usually learn about their emotions during their years in education. Certain areas are seen as vital, but emotional intelligence is a new thing.

This means that the early relationship that was formed with one's emotions will generally be carried into one's adult years, and it won't matter if this relationship was healthy or unhealthy.

The Relationship

So coming back to this early relationship, there can be two ways that one can develop in order to cope with one's emotions. This will generally depend on how one's caregivers responded to one's emotions as a child and to their own emotions.

Emotional Regulation

Here, a child will develop the ability to regulate their emotions; this means that they will rarely act on them, or simply deny that they exist and repress them. They will be able to just be with them, without getting too caught up in them. If they become too overwhelming, the child will learn that it is safe to seek assistance from others.

Emotional Dysregulation

In this case, the child will not develop the ability to regulate their emotions. This means that the child will have to either act on them or to deny and repress them. They won't be able to just be with them and will end up being caught up in them. And during times of being overwhelmed, they are unlikely to feel safe asking for assistance.

Empathic and Unempathic

The first example will relate to a caregiver that is empathic and the second example is for a caregiver that is unempathic. An empathic caregiver is emotionally available and will generally mirror, match, hold, and soothe their child during emotional distress.

And an unempathic caregiver is likely to be emotional unviable. So this means that they generally won't mirror, match, hold, or soothe their child during emotional distress.

These are just general guidelines, as there is likely to be moments where it won't be this black and white. However, this creates an idea about what it is like.

Consequences

As a result of the above taking place, it is likely to lead to completely different consequences. If as a child, one learned to regulate their emotions (through having an empathic caregiver), it is likely to mean that one will have a tendency to either self-regulate one's emotions or seek support in other people.

And if as a child, one didn't learn how to regulate their emotions (through having an unempathic caregiver), it is likely to mean that they will have a tendency of either repressing their emotions or of acting on them.

Repression

So the first child is rarely going to have to repress their emotions and this means that when this child grows into an adult, there shouldn't be the need to repress them either.

But the second child, who has had to repress their emotions, will likely grow into an adult that continues to repress their emotions. And this is inevitably going to lead to an emotional build-up within the body.

These emotions will have accumulated from when one was a child and may include all of the emotions that one has experienced as an adult, but denied and ignored.

Different Types Of Repression

For some people, this will involve certain moments as a child where they were abandoned, ignored, rejected, humiliated, felt hopeless, helpless, suicidal, guilty, and ashamed, for instance.

These can relate to the odd occasion or even experiencing these things on a daily or consistent basis. This can also include traumatic moments where one was: physically, emotionally or intellectually abused as a child.

And due to these moments taking place many years ago, they are generally blocked from the mind. But the body remembers these feelings and will not be silenced until they are recognised. This creates a heavy burden on the body and can result in a loss of energy.

Emotionally Trapped

In the beginning these may have only been emotions or feelings, but as time has gone on, they have become emotional states and have completely taken over: as when one weed appears and, soon after, the whole patch is covered in weeds.

The fact that there were only one or two weeds to begin with is hard to comprehend and finding the original weed or weeds can then become extremely difficult. Here one no longer feels one or two emotions, but has become emotionally trapped, with a general feeling of being overwhelmed or depressed.

Two Scenarios

It could be that one has felt this way their whole life or that one has felt this way after a certain experience. This could be the result of some kind of loss or traumatic occurrence that triggered emotions that have been trapped and frozen in the body for so long.

For the first person, this may be experienced as normal and how life is, simply because they have never felt any different. For the other person, however, it might not feel normal. This could be due to the fact that these feelings have been repressed for so many years, causing a disconnection to occur.

Awareness

Perhaps one has recognised the connection between how they felt as a child and how they feel as adult, or simply realised that they need to be assisted emotionally.

Chapter 16

Emotional Body

While it is clear that one has a physical body, what might not be as clear is that one also has an emotional body. So much attention has been placed on the mind, or what could be called the mental body, that emotions are often seen as being insignificant, appearing only when one has certain thoughts.

This often creates the impression that emotions are just an effect of how one does or doesn't think. Based on this outlook, one's mind is in control and emotions are at the mercy of one's thoughts.

If one was to go along with this theory and adhere to the perspective that their thoughts are in control, then it will be vital that one 'masters' their mind. And if one's thoughts appear to create their feelings, what else could someone do?

In order to change something, it is often said that one needs to go to the root of the problem. With thoughts being seen as the cause, it is only natural that one would place their attention solely on the mind.

A Deeper Look

However, just because something has been around for a while, is believed by a lot of people, or is something that 'experts' or authority figures stand by, it doesn't mean that it is the truth. What is seen as correct at one point in time can be seen as completely inaccurate at another time.

Thoughts can define how one feels; to think about a beach is generally going to make one feel different than if they were to think about their house being destroyed. Yet while this is true, one's feelings can also play a part in how they think.

Emotional Beings

To hear that humans are emotional beings that think might sound out of place. What might sound more accurate would be to say that we are thinking beings that feel. As much as one might want to see oneself as acting through logic or reason, behaviour is generally the result of how we feel.

After this, the mind gets involved and creates some kind of logical reason or justification for how one has behaved. But no matter what the mind comes up with, emotions are the real driving forces behind our actions.

Impact

So not only can our emotional body influence how we think, it can also have an impact on our physical body. And yet through a lack of awareness when it comes to emotions and the effect they have, dis-ease is generally seen as being a consequence of one's DNA, for instance.

But just because one is unaware of something, it doesn't mean that it is not having an effect on one's life. Emotions can be ignored and dismissed when it comes to physical health and yet that doesn't mean that one is immune to their effects.

Emotional Problems

One thing that could make one want to heal their emotional body is by suffering emotional problems. But even if one doesn't think that they have emotional problems, they might find that they behave in ways that are dysfunctional and that their mind is out of control.

These two things might appear to have nothing to do with how one feels and yet how one feels can be the cause of what is going on in their mind and how they behave. For example, if one is experiencing emotions that are not too pleasant, one way of dealing with them (in the short term) is to obsessively think about something or to become addicted to doing something.

By doing this, the mind is regulating how one feels. And if these feelings weren't there, one wouldn't need to become obsessed with ideas or fantasies, or become addicted to people or rituals, because their emotional body would be at ease.

Different Areas

Although it can seem as though emotions are only experienced in one part of one's body or even that their mind is creating these emotions, each emotion that one feels is experienced in a different area of the body.

The chest area is where one can feel: abandonment, rejection, grief, sadness, and loss. Above the stomach one can feel: hopelessness, powerlessness, shame, loss of control, and death. Further down, in the stomach, is where guilt can be felt, and then, in one's hips, fear can be felt.

There are other emotions based in other places; these are some of the main areas.

Trapped Emotions

So while one can feel guilt when they have gone against their own values, or feel rejected when a relationship ends and then gradually settle down, it is also possible for someone to end up being stuck emotionally.

To constantly feel guilty, rejected, or even ashamed, or to feel this way in certain environments, will cause one to suffer. When one ends up being emotionally stuck, it can be the result of having trapped emotions in their body.

Causes

One of the biggest reasons why someone has trapped emotions in their body is because they have experienced some kind of trauma. As their feelings were not processed, they then stayed in the body. This could relate to: childhood abuse, the loss of a loved one, or a car accident.

The Usual Approach

When it comes to dealing with the emotional body and releasing these emotions, enabling one to become emotionally free, a masculine approach is not what is needed. This approach is all about doing and not being.

When one feels down about something, it is common for people to suggest: stay positive, keep your head up, or that you should just 'let go', amongst other things. And while this would work if it related to problems physical in nature, emotions are not physical things.

The mind can repress or deny what is too painful to face. But this is unlikely to deal with how one feels; it is simply avoidance. These emotions can then end up being trapped in one's body and control one's whole life.

The Mind

While the mind can live in a fantasy world and pretend that everything is fine, one's body, as well as one's relationships, will reveal exactly what is going on for someone. As Alice Miller once said, the body doesn't lie, whereas the mind can be full of lies and illusions.

One problem with today's world is that we often ignore the body and only listen to what the mind has to say. The truth is then ignored and what is not true becomes the truth. This includes the world at large and our own personal lives.

Awareness

So if the trapped emotions are not dealt with through doing or through force, how are they dealt with? They have to be faced and felt and as this is done, they will gradually be released. This is unlikely to be something that happens overnight and could take a while.

Chapter 17

Emotionally Dependent

As human beings, we are interdependent and although one can come to the conclusion that they are independent, this is just an illusion. They may well be able to support themselves financially, but they are still reliant on other people paying them their money.

This is clearly different to one being dependent on others for money. In this instance, it is a one-way process and one is not giving anything in return. When one is being paid for what they give, a mutual exchange is taking place.

This is a sign that one has developed oneself to a certain degree, and can give and receive in this area of their life. To be able to receive through giving is going to make one feel empowered and important.

That is, unless they are doing something that they don't enjoy. In this case, even though they are getting paid, they might not feel too empowered about it at the end of each day or week. In some cases, this might make them want to be paid for doing nothing, as they are so fed up with getting paid for doing what they don't enjoy.

Emotions

And while one is interdependent on others when it comes to making money, the same applies to one's emotional security. In order for one to feel emotionally secure and centred, it will be important to have support around oneself.

This is generally going to include: friends, family, colleagues, and a partner or lover. Each of these people will play an important role in how one feels, with some playing a bigger role than others.

Here, one will feel emotionally nurtured and nourished through spending time with these figures and simply having them in their life. And as one is receiving this from others, they will also give this in return.

Give And Take

This process is about giving and taking; it is not one-sided. These relationships could be described as interdependent and not dependent. This means that although one's emotional state is enhanced by being around these people from time to time, it is not completely defined by them.

One still has a sense of emotional autonomy, and this allows them to be by themselves and away from people without a sense of inner unrest. Unless one is facing some kind of loss, for instance, when there will naturally be a greater need to have other people around.

A Metaphor

A metaphor for this sense of interdependence would be the way in which one can go about their day once they have had something to eat. Food is unlikely to be on one's mind once one has eaten: one can focus properly on the task at hand. After a while, once hunger returns, one will think about food once more and take the steps to have it.

The Absence

When interdependence doesn't exist, one will find it hard to be away from someone or from a certain group of people. So to continue the metaphor of eating and food, it would be as if one has eaten and then experienced distress until eating again, one's mind being consumed with all kinds of thoughts and the need to eat again being extremely high.

These persons' emotional state will be completely defined by what is taking place externally, lacking the ability to regulate or soothe themselves from the inside.

Space

Each of us is going to want to have our own space and to do our own thing, and so it is going to be impossible for one to always be around the same person or people all the time.

Space is needed and after a while of being apart, one will want to come together once again. For someone who is emotionally dependent on another, this natural need to separate is going to be a challenge.

The Experience

So to return to the example from above: to be away from someone temporarily will not be like a regular relationship with food, in which one eats and has a break from eating, before eating again sometime later. It will be like eating once and then coming to the conclusion that one won't ever eat again.

There is naturally going to be a lot of anxiety and fear involved for this person, along with potentially feeling: abandoned, alone, cut off, or rejected, and perhaps feeling powerless, hopeless, or that one is going to die.

Confusion

Now, as one is physically separate and doesn't need to rely on anyone in particular in order to survive, this whole experience could be confusing. Physically one is not going to die if they are away from someone, but their emotional experience could make them feel as though they are going to die.

So if one's physical age is overlooked and one just takes into account what is going on emotionally, they will soon see that there is a big difference. What they could see is that they still feel like baby or a small child.

Childhood

As a baby and for a few years after, as a child, one is emotionally dependent on one's caregiver/s. The ideal is for one to eventually break away from caregivers, and to experience oneself as being physically separate. Through this process, one will develop the ability to manage one's emotions.

For this to take place, one will need to have a caregiver who is emotionally aware and in tune. If they are out of touch, there will be a greater chance of this process being sabotaged. A common result of having a caregiver who is emotionally cut off is that one's emotions will not be regulated or mirrored, through the caregiver being either physically or emotionally absent.

Separation

When this process doesn't take place, one is then unable to complete this important part of their development. One can end up being stuck at this stage and will then continue to see others as they saw their caregivers.

It will then be necessary for one to emotionally separate from one's caregivers as an adult; as one does this, they will find they are able to maintain an inner balance and a sense of consistency when other people are not around.

Awareness

The above is just one potential reason as to why one is emotionally dependent. If one still feels like they did as a child when people are not around, then they may have an emotional build-up.

Chapter 18

Emotionally Disconnected

While emotions are often seen as a distraction and an inconvenience, they are a vital part of being human. Without them, life would be pretty meaningless and while there wouldn't be any lows, there also wouldn't be any highs.

It would lead to a life that is very empty and although one might be alive, it would be nothing more than a life of simply existing or surviving. So this could be a life that makes one wonder if life is really worth living.

An Analogy

When one goes to sleep, they typically lay on a bed that is comfortable and soft. This allows them to relax and to have the potential of a good night's sleep. Their body can connect to the bed, without needing to retract or tense up. Quite simply, they can let go and just be.

If they were to sleep on concrete or on a wood floor, the experience wouldn't be the same. Here, one may feel tense and uptight, and pain is likely to arise. If this person was to let go and just be, they would probably feel worse than if they maintained a closed position.

A Matter Of Degree

This example is, in many ways, what it can be like for someone who is emotionally disconnected. There is not much comfort or pleasure to be had; what there is likely to be is a sense of being cut off and that something is missing. How disconnected one is will often define how one does or doesn't experience life.

One could feel disconnected at certain times in their life and so don't see it as a problem. It could be seen as a minor issue and so it is overlooked.

There can, however, be other people who feel completely disconnected and it therefore doesn't matter where they are or who they are with. One could come to the conclusion that they are cut off or they could have been in this position for so long, that they are unaware of life being any different.

It's Normal

If emotional development and awareness were part of the education system or society in general, then one would have a way of not only knowing that they are disconnected, but also find it easy to come across solutions to this challenge.

However, as emotions are generally ignored in today's world, it means that there is rarely anything external that will supply one with the feedback they need to see that something is not right. By lacking this external mirror or catalyst, one can end up coming to the conclusion that what they are going through is normal and simply how life is.

When it comes to one's physical health, there are plenty of things around to show someone that if they have a certain symptom, something is not right, but the same approach is not available when it comes to emotional challenges.

Extreme Highs

One thing that someone can do when they feel emotionally disconnected is to engage in pursuits that will give them an extreme high. The problem is that while these work, they don't last; before long one is back to where they started, and this could mean one is back to feeling numb.

Here, one could take part in some kind of extreme sport, pushing their body to its limits in order to feel something. Similarly, one could become hooked on going to the gym to feel that rise in their life. Sex is another option that can give one an instant experience of feeling something.

In much the same way, getting tattoos - whilst temporarily painful - allows one to feel something. There are also drugs, drink, and food, and these all have the potential to give one an emotional high.

Consequences

When one is not experiencing these highs and artificially getting in touch with their feelings, there are going to be all kinds of consequences that can arise as a result of being emotionally disconnected.

One of these can be a disconnection from one's body, which can feel separate from them. What it does or doesn't do is then random and out of one's control. Along with this physical disconnection can be the experience of being separate from people, leaving one feeling alone and isolated. One could find themselves saying yes to things they would rather not do and being in situations they would rather not be in.

One's needs, wants, and desires can also be a mystery to oneself; knowing when one is hungry or tired can be a challenge. It could well be possible that one has plenty of friends, but it is less likely that they will have relationships that are deep or intimate. Relationships are likely to be superficial and without any kind of depth.

To be out of touch with how one feels will mean that one is oblivious to the effects that their feelings are having. So what shows up in their life and how people respond to them will appear random, as one won't be able to see the connection between the inner and outer world.

Causes

When one lives in their head and is estranged from their body, is a clear sign that one is carrying a certain amount of emotional pain, and that this emotional pain has become trapped in the body.

This could be the result of experiences in adult life, and also go back to what happened to one as a baby and a child. It could even have been a one-off event that was traumatic or an accumulation of events that, while seemingly insignificant at the time, were just as traumatic.

One may have been brought up by a caregiver who was emotionally out of touch with themselves and therefore couldn't provide the attunement or empathy required to raise an emotionally healthy child.

Trapped Emotions

So as there was no external mirror to validate and regulate how one felt, one had to simply push their feelings and emotions outside of their awareness. At that age, one wouldn't have had the ability to deal with them oneself.

Over time their body would have become a place of pain and living in their head would have provided an escape. But although it enabled one to avoid pain, this process also resulted in them being cut off from every other emotion.

Awareness

The above is a rough guideline of what can happen. Emotions and feelings that have remained trapped in one's body need to be released in order for one to regain their connection to their body and to their emotions.

Chapter 19

Emotional Instability

While having emotional stability is the ideal, it is not something that everyone can relate to. But this doesn't mean that the people who do experience emotional stability are always stable and go through life unscathed.

To be human means that we are emotional beings and so unless one has become emotionally numb and cut off, they are going to experience emotional ups and downs. This is part of life and not something one should try to deny.

If one is in touch with both sides of their emotional spectrum, they will have moments of feeling good and of feeling not so good. Their reason for feeling down or low might be because they have experienced some kind of loss.

And loss, either through the loss of a person or perhaps a certain position that one had, will cause one to experience inner instability. There will be certain ideas about how long the pain will last, but human beings respond differently, so this is not set in stone.

There are said to be five stages of grief, for instance, but how long these stages last for will vary from person to person. It is not always a linear process.

Stability

When one experiences emotional instability during moments of loss and a mild sense of instability at other times, they can be seen as fairly adjusted human beings. They are emotionally together and do not suffer from emotional instability as a way of life.

This is likely to mean that their behaviour is fairly consistent, simply because how they feel inside is generally the same. How they dress could also reflect this inner harmony and therefore stop them from looking unkempt.

Their ability to plan and organise is also going to be good. To do this, one needs to be able to think clearly and when emotions are settled, this will naturally be a lot easier. It could be assumed that these people have less stress than others and that this is why they are calmer.

There could be an element of truth to this, but what it also comes down to is the fact that they are more resilient. Challenges will appear and yet they are able to weather the storms and not let it affect them to a strong degree. So instead of making a mountain out of a molehill, things will generally be kept in proportion.

Balance

This is going to allow one to feel a sense of balance and enable the mind and emotions to work together. And if one has always experienced life this way, it will be hard for them to comprehend what it must be like for someone who doesn't experience life in the same way.

For people who only know what it feels like to be emotionally unstable, the above might sound like some kind of dream. They may have come to the conclusion that life will always be this way for them.

Instability

There are different degrees of instability: for some people, this will be something that defines their whole life, while for others, it may just appear during certain situations. But no matter when, where, or how much it happens, it is going to create challenges for someone.

Being able to have a sense of inner balance and harmony is going to be a problem. Mood swings will be something they are familiar with and their behaviour is going to reflect this. One moment they may feel up and good about themselves and the next minute they are down and can't bear to be in their own company.

This could take place from time to time or be a regular occurrence. And this means that their ability to plan and to organise is going to be affected also. Erratic and impulsive behaviour could be what they are used to and this could lead to a whole host of problems.

Consequences

For some people this may result in them overspending or overeating. One minute they might be pleasant and the next moment they might be unpleasant and even hostile. Plans might be made and then cancelled at the last minute.

Emotionally, one may have become accustomed to feeling depressed and then know that before long, they will be full of life and ready to take on the world. This person's style of dress could fluctuate to reflect their inner instability. These are just some examples and there are many others.

What Is Going On?

When one is like this, they may end up being labelled as having some kind of disorder. This could then result in them forming a certain identity and as having a borderline personality or being bipolar.

Some people say this is due to genetics and others say it's due to what happened during childhood. Perhaps there is some truth in both views. However, what is perfectly clear is that when someone is suffering from emotional instability, they haven't got the ability to regulate their emotions.

Emotional regulation

This doesn't exist for them and this causes their emotions to be completely out of control. It is a bit like a traffic light, which allows the traffic to be controlled rather than to come through all at once. Without the lights, all the traffic would go at once and there would be nothing but accidents and near collisions.

Traffic lights regulate the traffic and when it comes to a human being, having this inner ability stops one from being overwhelmed and taken out by their emotions. As this ability is so vital, it can seem strange that one wouldn't have it.

Childhood

Having a caregiver that is empathic and aware is also vital, but this doesn't always take place either. When this is absent, it can cause one to grow up without the ability to regulate oneself.

As a baby and a young child, one doesn't have the ability to regulate how they feel. This means that one is completely dependent on one's caregiver and the people around oneself at that time to regulate how one feels.

Now, if this is a caregiver that is empathic and available in most cases, one is likely to be fine. Through being regulated by one's caregiver, one will soon internalise this ability and the brain will develop in the right way.

But when a caregiver is not available enough, or is more or less completely absent, this ability won't form and one is left to deal with one's emotions alone. Not only will the individual not develop this ability, but they will also have to disconnect from their emotions in order to avoid the emotional pain in order to survive.

Trapped Emotions

These emotions will have stayed trapped in the body, and so they will not only have to deal with present emotions that arise, but also cope with emotional build-up from the past.

It won't be like a rain drop; it will be like a tidal wave. As these have built up for so long, it won't be much of a surprise for someone to have so many ups and downs. A rain drop won't do very much, but if these rain drops are to build up over many years, there could be far more damage; the same clearly applies to one's emotional build-up.

Awareness

There will be two things that need to happen here. The first is that one will need to release the trapped emotions from their emotional body, and the second is that one will need to develop the ability to regulate oneself.

Chapter 20

Emotional Regulation

Although emotions and feelings are something each one of us has, it doesn't mean that they are easy to handle or manage. For some people, they generally don't cause too many problems, unless there is a major challenge in their life.

And then there are other people who find it incredibly difficult to cope with their emotions. It is then irrelevant as to what is or what is not going on in their life, as the consequences are the same. Here, one can end up being completely controlled by emotions and feel forever at their mercy.

Now, if these emotions were 'positive' and uplifting, then there is not going to be much concern as to whether one is controlled by them or not. This would be something that one is likely to embrace and not resist. What makes this a challenge is when these emotions are far from pleasant and are what could be labelled as destructive.

In the first example, one is generally able to regulate how they feel. And so they have a reasonable degree of emotional control. But when it comes to my next example, this ability doesn't exist. Or, if it does, it is not developed enough for one to handle one's emotions.

Two Extremes

There are going to be people who have this ability, which allows them to minimize any emotional turbulence they may experience in life; however, there are others who feel completely powerless when they experience any kind of emotional unrest.

There will then be people who are more or less in-between the two. So it's not so much of a challenge that they feel out of control, but they won't exactly feel in control either. In this instance, this can relate to someone who has become numb.

To explore the two extremes, it would appear that one person has something the other person lacks. Both are human and are biologically the same, and yet, emotionally, they are very different.

Emotional Regulation

This gives one the ability to do at least two things. On one side, it makes it possible for one to just be with whatever emotions arise (in most cases); they don't have to deny how they are feeling and therefore repress them.

This also means that one won't necessarily have to act on how they feel all the time. One will be able to resist the urge to direct these emotions externally onto people or animals, for instance, who are innocent and have no part to play in one's emotional experience.

One is able to soothe oneself from the inside, as a mother would settle down her crying baby. If this is not possible, then one might seek the assistance of a trusted friend or a partner to hold the space for them. The main thing is that they are comfortable enough with their emotions to either soothe themselves and, if this is not possible, they will ask for support from others.

The Missing Ability

If this ability was the norm, then it is likely that many things in this world would be different. In reality, this ability is something that few people possess, and this leads to all kinds of consequences. Some of these can be overlooked and played down, while others cannot be missed and create clear destruction.

Consequences

To deny and cover up how one feels can lead to: dysfunctional relationships, illness, physical pain, and depression, amongst other things. To get caught up in how one feels could lead to reactive and impulsive behaviour.

One could end up buying things that they don't need, getting into relationships that are dysfunctional, and saying and doing things they will later come to regret. Drugs, sex, food, and alcohol could all be used as a way of regulating how one feels.

Being Human

Now, to be human means that one is imperfect, and that is normal and part of the human experience; it is not something to feel ashamed of. To deny how one feels or to act in a way that is destructive, is going to happen from time to time.

When one is experiencing intense stress due to a job coming to an end, the loss of someone close to oneself, or the end of a significant relationship, emotional regulation can give way to internal repression and external destruction. However, this will be a short-term challenge and not a way of life.

The challenge is when this is the only way that one knows and one has no idea how to regulate oneself. Denying how one feels or relying on external things to feel better could be the only approach one knows.

Causes

This is like owning a car, but not having a place to park it. In this case, one has emotions and what they don't have is a way to deal with them. Something is missing, and although it might always have been this way for someone, there is a reason for it; how one was cared for by their primary caregiver, as a baby and then as a child, will typically define whether one can emotionally regulate themselves or not as an adult.

Empathic And Unempathic

The ideal caregiver is one who is empathic and emotionally in tune with oneself. This will allow them to mirror, soothe, and validate what their child is feeling. At this age, the child has not developed the ability regulate how they feel, so the mother figure provides this until the child develops this ability.

Through this process taking place many, many times, the child will gradually internalise the mother's responses. As a result of this, they will develop the ability to regulate themselves and feel comfortable enough to ask another for emotional support.

If the mother is unempathic and out of tune with her own emotions, the child is going to pay the price (unless someone else fulfils this role instead). So the child would then have to deal with their own emotions and feelings at an age when they were not ready to do so.

Unless something is done during their adult years, this ability might never be developed. So as a result of the mother figure not providing this, one can end up looking outside for their entire lives.

Awareness

There is the potential for this ability to be developed in later life, if the commitment and support is there. What can stop one from being able to soothe oneself and to just be with one's emotions is when one has trapped feelings and emotions within their body.

And if one has never had the ability to regulate their emotions, it is inevitable that they will have built up. These will need to be released in order for one to settle down.

Chapter 21

Emotionally Stuck

It is often said that one's emotional age is not always the same as their biological age. This can be shown through one's feelings and seen through certain behaviours and reactions that people have.

One may even try to deny that they haven't grown up and justify their behaviour in some way. Here, one could say that they don't want to grow up or that life is all about having fun, for example.

On the other side of this are people who are very much aware of how old they feel. These people don't want to justify or rationalise how they are; they just want to grow up.

There are also people who are not aware of being emotionally stuck, simply because it is the only thing they know. It is normal and feels familiar to them, and can lead to all kinds of pain and suffering.

Three Options

In the first example, it is as if one has no awareness of their emotional age and therefore finds two options within life: either they stay where they are, or they grow up and experience life as being entirely about responsibility, hard work, and obligations.

The second person, however, can see that the option above is not the only one available. While they want to grow up, they know that life involves responsibilities and hard work, but also moments of adult play and fulfilment.

The third person is unlikely to enjoy their experience of life. Based on their perception of life and of themselves, though, it may appear as the only way life can be experienced.

Areas Of Life

Regardless of what one's position on their emotional age is, this is something that can affect every area of one's life, such as: self image, career, relationships, finances, and mental and emotional health.

It's Normal

There are a number of ways that one can come to the conclusion that they are emotionally stuck. One may come to this conclusion through: reading, being around someone who is emotionally developed, or through a general awareness that one has not grown up.

These insights are often hard to come by and this can be the result of emotional development being so rare in today's world.

It is often through comparison that people come to see if how they feel or what they are doing is right or wrong, or good or bad. There are also people who will not only look to others, but look within themselves to decide if they are on the right track and doing the right thing.

If one were to look to other people to assess whether they are emotionally undeveloped, in most cases they are unlikely to find a functional model to compare themselves with. That is unless they happen to have a certain role model, friend, or family member who is emotionally developed.

Influences

There are many influences here and some of the primary ones are: family, friends, teachers, the media, and popular culture. It is through these sources that one's emotional development can be set and whether or not one feels they are undeveloped or not.

Based on what these sources are often like, it will often be normal for one to stay in a regressed state unless one generally questions life or has the drive to grow. The media and popular culture generally don't encourage emotional development; in most cases, what they promote or idealise, is the result of emotional undevelopment.

It is through these role models, and subjects focused upon by the media, that one can come to the conclusion that how they feel is normal or how life is.

The Main Influence

However, the primary influence in whether one is emotionally developed or undeveloped is the childhood years. What happened during these years will play a massive role in one's emotional health.

Now for some people, emotional development can be slightly off, while for others, there can be the feeling of being extremely undeveloped. This can depend on the quality of nurturing that one received and whether one experienced any kind of trauma.

Empathic And Unempathic Care

And whether one had a caregiver that was primarily empathic or unempathic will often be the defining factor. An empathic caregiver is one who is generally emotionally available and in tune with the child's needs, whereas an unempathic caregiver is one who is generally emotionally unavailable and out of tune with the child's needs.

From the moment one is born, one will have certain mental and emotional needs. These will have to be met at the right time or else it will create problems later in life. If they are met, it will allow one to go onto the next stage of their development.

If they are not met, it can disable one from going on to the next stage of their development. Their physical body may change, but their emotional body can stay the same.

Life Goes On

And while one can feel emotionally stuck at the times their needs are not met, life carries on and doesn't stop just because one has emotionally stopped growing. This will inevitably lead to problems and to the creation of pain and suffering.

Even though life has continued at an emotional level, one can feel as though they have never left those moments of being a child. And this means that how they felt at those times, when their needs were not met, can be how they will feel as an adult, too.

Examples

Through regressing to this early time or just by merging with one's emotions, one can feel: rejected, abandoned, lost, empty, powerless, needy, desperate, hopeless, helpless, worthless, vulnerable, and overly sensitive.

This can then influence how one views oneself, other people, and life itself, as well as influencing the kind of people one is attracted to and attracts.

Frozen In Time

The emotional pain that was experienced as a child has remained in the body; it has been frozen or trapped there. And this means that in most cases, these emotional needs will not be able to be met as an adult.

As these emotions relate to childhood needs and wants, it will mean that they will just have to be released and let go. By feeling the feelings, they will begin to disappear and allow one to feel emotionally like an adult.

Trapped Emotions – How Are They Affecting Your life?

Chapter 22

Empathy

There are many different things that make someone human and therefore allow them to have a human experience; one of these things is empathy. This is something one can have for oneself and something that can extend outwards and towards other human beings.

It enables one to mirror another person's pain and what they are going through emotionally. While this could be towards an individual person, it could also go out towards a whole country or an area of a country.

One can also feel a general empathy towards animals, and feel what they are going through during their suffering as a result of other human beings or when they are receiving treatment for a wound, for example. In this sense, one can feel empathy towards just about anything on the planet.

For example, if someone is a tree surgeon or has lived around nature for all or most of their life, they might feel a connection to the trees around them. And so when they see trees cut down, they might feel a sense of pain or grief at what is taking place.

Different Levels

Now, not everyone on this planet has the same level of empathy: some people connect to what others are feeling, while others can have the same experience but without the same intensity.

There are also people on this planet who have no empathy whosever. And although some of these people are shut off and unlikely to cause too much harm to other human beings, there are others who are a threat to the people around them and even to the whole planet.

When it comes to these people, they are typically described as psychopaths. People who are extremely narcissistic can also act as if they have no empathy for anyone or anything.

Careers

When it comes to people who have empathy or a lack of it, their choice of career can vary. Of course there is going to be the potential for people who have it and those who lack it to work in the same kinds of environments.

However, there are also certain hotspots for people who have it and people who do not; some people, for instance, feel more empathy towards animals than they can towards humans.

This could cause someone to work with animals and be very caring and loving towards them. However, when it comes to humans, they might be seen as distant and uncaring, and can even act with a general disdain for the suffering of fellow human beings.

People with high levels of empathy could work as a: doctor, nurse, fireman, therapist, charity worker, personal trainer, artist, and vet, amongst other things.

People who have low levels of empathy can often be found in the corporate world or committing crimes, for instance. But while the actions of a criminal are easily observable, when it comes to what goes on in corporations, it can take a while to be known.

Making Decisions

In order for someone to do well in these kinds of environments or to take the life of another, in the case of a recognised criminal, it is rarely in their best interests to feel another's pain. To make a decision that is the best for the company, regardless of whether it will harm a few human beings or a few thousand, will be a lot easier if someone can't feel.

This is why it is often said that having emotional intelligence is rarely an asset in the world of business. While it may sound as though it would be, the ability to make quick decisions, and decisions that are in the interest of the company (rather than the people in it), is often all that matters.

Certain parts of the modern world are set up to support people who lack empathy. And yet there are also areas that support, nourish, and encourage empathy. As the saying goes: the world is made up of all of types of people.

The Heart

Different parts of the body have different uses and while the heart pumps blood around the body, it is also the place where empathy is experienced. Like most things in life, if something is not in balance, it naturally ends up being out of balance. One can have a shower and the water can be just right, but it could also be too hot or too cold.

And when it comes to empathy, the same thing can occur. For instance, one's heart could be closed or wide open, so that one can end up having no feeling or they can end up feeling too much.

119

Pain

The heart is where pain is felt and this can include: rejection, abandonment, loss, betrayal, and grief. There are three options that one can choose to take in order to deal with this pain. One is to repress it and to deny that it is there (no empathy); another is to stay stuck in the pain and to become overly sensitive (overly empathic); the final option is to seek the assistance of a therapist and process the pain (balanced empathy).

The way in which one deals with pain will often depend on the environment that they are in. So if one is an adult, it might be possible to seek the assistance of a therapist; that's if they feel safe enough to do so. On the other hand, if it is a child that is in pain, the option may not be there, as it does not feel safe enough.

Protection

This could be pain that one felt as an adult, having lost a family member or friend, or could be the pain one felt during childhood, as the result of being emotionally, physically, or verbally abused - or all three.

To protect themselves from the pain that they were experiencing, they shut down all feelings and through this process their heart gradually began to close. At the time it wasn't about one consciously choosing to lose their empathy; it was simply a matter of survival.

Through one being around people who were like this, the only loving things around them may have been animals. This can be why some people feel more empathy towards animals than towards humans.

Trapped Emotions

So these emotions and feelings from the moment or moments that were traumatic remain in one's heart and other organs within the body. And while the heart might be functioning normally at a biological level, its other functions - such as allowing one to feel - are not working.

One is operating in life without it and is no longer a whole human being; they might be responding to life intellectually and through their body's needs, drives, and instincts, but their heart is out of action.

Awareness

This is not to say that if someone has no empathy it is always because of trapped emotions and feelings. However, if one has an emotional build-up within them, a natural consequence of that is to shut down emotionally.

So if one has difficulty showing empathy or has too much, it might be a sign that they have trapped emotions and feelings that need to be released.

Chapter 23

Energy

In one way or another, life is all about energy; it is what creates and supports life and it also leads to movement and motion. Without it, nothing would exist or survive, and nothing would ever happen or change.

As human beings, we are no different. Whether it involves: getting out of bed, going to work, doing exercise or sport, achieving certain goals or dreams, or anything else for that matter, energy is incredibly important.

To function at a high level or even a basic level requires energy and plenty of it. When one feels that they have energy, anything can seem possible, and when one doesn't have energy, just about everything can seem impossible.

The Usual Approach

If someone feels low on energy, the typical approach is to seek a change in diet, have more sleep, for one to exercise if they don't already, and, if they do, more exercise may be recommended.

As well as eating different things and cutting back on others, there may also be the addition of certain supplements. These can be vitamins, minerals, and protein powders, for instance.

In extreme cases where these solutions don't work, one may even be labelled as having some kind of physical or mental challenge. One of these is often called chronic fatigue syndrome, and depression can be another.

Popular Choices

For many years there have been different kinds of energy drinks. In the beginning these were often used for someone who was involved in some kind of exercise. As time has gone by, they have become consumed not only for exercise, but for any moment when one feels thirsty or wants an energy boost.

There are also different snacks and treats that can be bought as a way to perk someone up. Some of these could be described as healthy and some of these could be seen as unhealthy.

What stands out about energy drinks is how popular they have become in such a short space of time. For some people, these drinks will be an addiction and something they need in order to function.

Reasons

There are, inevitably, numerous reasons as to why so many people feel that they don't have enough energy. It could be due to what I have said above, but it could also be the result of one not having a fulfilling life. Life may feel like a chore and not cause one to feel inspired or feel that it is even worthwhile.

One thing that is often overlooked - at least in mainstream culture - is emotional repression and the effects that this can have on one's energy and wellbeing.

Emotions

Emotions are often ignored and overlooked in today's world. And if one doesn't form a healthy relationship with them as a child, it may mean that one never will. As the education system generally doesn't educate people on them, it will often depend on whether one educates oneself in later life.

Emotions are invisible to the naked eye and can't be caught or put into a box. As the western world is primarily focused on all that is physical and seen by the eye, emotions are often seen as problems that simply need to be removed.

By emotions being perceived in this way, the typical approach is to deny that they exist and to repress them.

Out Mind Out Of Sight

The mind can use a myriad of defence mechanisms in order to avoid facing emotions. And what they will generally lead to is emotional repression. Over time, the mind can forget all about these emotions.

They then no longer exist and that is the end of it, as far as the mind is concerned. But while this may seem accurate and even be beneficial in the short term, these emotions have not gone. All that has happened is that the mind has lost contact with them.

The Body

To the mind, everything is then back to normal, and there is nothing to worry about. However, this is nothing more than an illusion that the mind forms. Metaphorically speaking, the mind can feel like the storm is over and yet the body is right in the middle of the storm.

These emotions have to go somewhere and the body has plenty of places where they can be absorbed; one's muscles, bones, skin, and vital organs can all carry the burden. This is, of course, unnatural and not what they are meant to do.

But if one's mind doesn't want to face emotion, then the body won't have much choice. The natural tendency of the body is to release and let go of emotions, but this process can be blocked by the mind.

Consequences

This can lead to physical discord and cause the body to be out of balance. And as it can't undertake its natural process of releasing emotions, it is inevitable that unhealthy consequences will take place.

What happens to the body can depend on how long repression has gone on for and how much repression has taken place. For some people, this will include moments that were moderately painful, to moments that were extremely traumatic, with emotional pain that originated in one's younger years, to emotional pain experienced as an adult.

Awareness

Here the body can become heavy, sluggish and diseased. And when this becomes too much, the mind will no longer be able to deny or ignore these emotions. At first they may have been the equivalent of a few rains drops, but over time they have become a tidal wave. Here, one can feel trapped, overwhelmed, and without energy.

Chapter 24

False Self

Many names have been used over the years when it comes to describing the part of someone that is not real or authentic. One of those names is the false self, but many others have also been used, such as: the mask that someone wears, the pseudo self, and adaptive behaviour, for instance.

These descriptions and many others describe what has been formed on top of the real or true self. But there is also opposition out there to the concept of the true self, with some people taking the position that no such thing exists. And this point of view is supported by the outlook that people are constantly changing and that behaviour can change depending on one's environment.

The Illusion

So through these changes taking place in ways that are seemingly insignificant and sometimes significant, the true self is seen as an illusion. Yet if someone is looking for something within that is fixed and never changes, then the true self is surely going to be seen as nothing more than a phrase that sounds good.

This could the mean that a false self doesn't exist either, and that one is simply behaving in ways that they have chosen. In this case, human beings would be nothing more than machines that have nothing going on within, instead being completely dependent on what the external world expects of them.

And while one is going to be influenced by what is going on in the external world and by the people that they associate with, it doesn't mean that they are therefore a blank slate within.

Changeable

Everything on this planet is in a constant state of change and nothing ever stays the same. And the true self is not something that is always the same and unaffected by life. How someone saw themselves at age twelve is generally going to be different to how they see themselves when they are or were twenty-two.

This is to be expected and is a sign that they have grown and developed as a human being. However, just because someone can look back on their life and see that they have changed, it doesn't mean that this change reflects what is true for them.

It could be an identity that they have become accustomed to, one that gains the approval and acceptance of others, or it could be one that leads to their innermost needs and wants being fulfilled (in most cases).

True Self

Here, one would act in ways that lead to them getting their needs and wants met. And these needs and wants are inevitably going to change over time and this means that how one defines their true self will also change.

It would also lead to one generally having people in their life who mirror how they see themselves. So some relationships that one has are going to last for a long time and others are going to burn out before too long.

One perspective is that this is down to a lack of loyalty or that one is unstable. But from another point of view, this could simply show that how one sees oneself has now changed and, as a result of this, the relationship no longer validates who they are. So, as the other person has stayed the same, one no longer feels the same connection.

Comfortable

And just because someone doesn't change externally, it doesn't mean that their identity is causing them to be happy and fulfilled in life. One could have the same friends for years or not change how they come across, and yet this could be nothing more than a mask.

The roles they play have become so familiar and comfortable that they have come to the conclusion that that is who they really are. But while these roles may feel comfortable and a safe way to live, they are nothing more than false selves.

False Self

So if the true self is the result of one listening to one's wants, needs, desires, and preferences, then the false self would be the opposite of this. One's point of focus would be on the external world, and in doing what would lead to gaining the acceptance of others.

One's point of focus would be on pleasing other people and making sure they do not step out of line. And this doesn't have to relate simply to strangers and people that one doesn't know very well; it can also include one's friends, family, and acquaintances.

What is going on in one's body could be a mystery, with their attention being stuck in their head. So one's focus is then not on the inner world and what is true for them, but on the outer world, what is true for others, and what one thinks other people expect from them.

Trapped Emotions

What can stop one from getting into their body and becoming aware of their true needs and wants is emotional build-up. One can end up living on the surface of oneself.

These trapped feelings and emotions can form a false self and through these feelings' power, one can lose all self-control and the ability to make conscious choices that will reflect one's true wants and needs.

So how one sees oneself and how one behaves around others can be defined by trapped emotions and feelings: as can their thoughts, feelings, and what they say around others. This is likely to happen automatically and one can end up feeling as though this false self is who they really are.

Awareness

The emotional build-up can be due to what has happened in one's adult life and go back to when one was a child. As their emotions were not allowed to be expressed during the moments when they appeared, it meant that they stayed in one's body.

And like parasites, they took over and infiltrated one's experience of life. These will need to be released and as this is done, one will be able to let go of their false self.

Chapter 25

Feeling Good

There is something that just about everyone wants, and that is to feel good. It plays a big part in what someone does and doesn't do. This can relate to one feeling emotionally centred and at ease internally, and/or through having a heightened sense of wellbeing due to what is taking place externally.

In the first example, it is likely that one will feel good because of what is going on internally and yet as we are interdependent, external events are also likely to play a part.

When it is due to the second example, one may feel good about their life in general or have the experience because of a certain occurrence; it won't necessarily be due to what is taking place internally.

But if one feels a deep sense of unhappiness within, it is going to be a challenge to feel good. It won't matter what is going on externally and where one is in the world or what they are doing. How one feels on the inside might be pushed to one side for a while, but it is unlikely to just disappear.

Options

There are common options for people to choose from when they don't feel good; some of these are fairly functional, and others can be dysfunctional if they are relied upon. Things like alcohol, drugs, food, and sex, are all recognised as being used to alter how one feels.

If these were used from time to time - excluding drugs - it is probably not going to cause too many problems. To use these in excess, however, is going to lead to the creation of further problems and one could end up feeling even worse.

Exercise

Engaging in some kind of exercise every now and then is good way to alter how one feels. One will get fitter, change how they look, and the chemicals in their brain will also change. So there are many levels to this and one can benefit in many ways.

However, exercise is only going to get one so far and this could become another form of avoidance. Once they have stopped working out or doing a certain exercise, they are likely to return to how they were feeling.

Diet

Another approach would be for one to change what they are eating and to get the right nutrients into the body. This may also involve taking certain vitamins and minerals as a way to supplement what they are eating.

As today's food is not as good as it used to be, in terms of nutritional value, there is a strong chance that one is lacking something. So to eat or to take the right things is going to change how one feels. However, it might not be enough.

Drugs

There are drugs that one can use to alter their mental state that are classed as legal, and others that are seen as illegal. The illegal drugs that people use have been around for years and although their names may change, the drug itself rarely does.

Antidepressants are commonly used to treat people who have emotional problems. The trouble with these is that they don't actually deal with these emotions and can cause one to be completely cut off from how they feel.

So they could end up feeling like a zombie, completely out of touch with themselves. Or they could end up coming across as constantly happy and inauthentic; so that they are depressed, yet happy about it.

Low

When someone feels down or low, this could be an experience that they have always had or it could have been something that has recently come about. If one has always experienced life this way, then they are not going to know what it is like to experience life in another way.

But if one felt fine before or only had moments of feeling bad, and then they end up feeling low as a way of life, they are going to be able to see that there is another way. This can give them hope and the conviction that they can return to how they were once again.

Trapped Emotions

Now, there could be all kinds of reasons as to why one doesn't feel good and one of these reasons is due to trapped emotions. There will be two levels to this; not only will one feel different as a result of having them stuck in their body, but their body will also respond differently.

It could be said that as their body is responding differently, one will feel different. And while this is true, it can also be the other way around, with how one feels shaping what is going on in the body.

The Body

It might seem inaccurate to mention the body and not the mind, especially as the mind is meant to be in charge of how one feels. But while the mind has generally been seen as the organ that affects how one feels, recent evidence has shown that this is not actually the case.

It is what is going on in one's stomach that is defining how one feels and not what is going on in one's head; what is happening in one's mind is often the result of what is going on in their stomach. It has been said that over ninety percent of serotonin and over fifty percent of dopamine is made in the stomach.

So this means that one can change their thoughts and 'think positive', but if their stomach is not in order, it might not make any difference.

Emotions

And while emotions can be held all over the body, the most important area, and the one that will define how one feels, will be just above the stomach. This is sometimes called the enteric brain, the ego, or the reptilian complex. In the heart can be loss, abandonment, grief, betrayal, and rejection, and these will need to be dealt with.

And yet these will be on top of what is happening just above one's stomach. In this area can be the following feelings: powerlessness, hopelessness, loss of control, and death.

Disruption

What these trapped emotions will do is disrupt the body and stop it from functioning as it should. And when that happens, how one feels is going to change. These trapped emotions could relate to what has happened in one's adult years and go back to when they were a baby and a child.

So one may have forgotten about what happened and yet the emotional experiences have stayed inside the body.

Awareness

These trapped emotions will need to be released and then one can see if this is the reason why they feel as they do.

Chapter 26

Feeling Safe

Although each one of us has a body, it doesn't mean that everyone feels that it is safe to be in their body. It might even sound confusing as to how this could be, as one's body is a big part of who they are.

Instead of one being in their body, what they can end up doing is living in their head. This is not something that one usually chooses to do at conscious level; it is something that can happen as a result of certain experiences occurring in their life.

To be stuck in one's head is one experience that someone can have, as is the experience of being outside one's body. This is typically described as dissociation and this can create the illusion of being outside of oneself.

Two Options

But whether it is being in one's head, outside one's body, or both, depending on the situation, it is not going to make life very enjoyable. It can cause one to be cut off from their emotions and unable to use them to manage their life.

Or one could go to the other extreme as a rule or at certain times, and become consumed by emotions and feelings. When this happens, it will be more or less impossible to think properly and to do such things as: planning, organising, and being on time for meetings or appointments.

One is then stuck in their emotional brain or in their survival brain, instead of being able to use the two together, along with their thinking brain.

Home

While as human beings we often live in a house or flat that we call our home, there is another place that is our true home; without one feeling at home in their body, it is likely to be a real challenge to feel at home anywhere.

The disconnection that one can have with their own body is also going to be experienced as an outer disconnection. What is going on internally is going to be reflected in one's external reality. This can then go on to include the feeling that one doesn't belong on the planet.

So having the feeling of being supported or connected to the earth is not going to be there or, if it is there, will not be a consistent experience. Instead, one can feel cut off from life and as if their head is in the clouds.

An Observer

Here, one won't experience life as a participator; they will experience life as an observer, nothing more than a bystander who is looking in from the outside. To be an observer is, of course, an important ability to have, but is not practical as a way of life.

Life may then be something that one can't fully engage with and embrace. What it is for this person is something that they must endure and face. Survival is something that they can relate to and thriving is then nothing more than a fancy word.

Needs

One might be able to become aware of their needs and wants during certain times, but to be able to do this on a consistent basis, one needs to live in their body. So instead of one knowing what one truly needs and wants, one can end up being caught up in other people's need and wants.

This is often classed as being a people-pleaser or an approval-seeker. But if one doesn't feel safe in their body it means that they don't feel safe being themselves - and so following others can appear to be the only safe option available.

All Areas

This doesn't just include big decisions that one makes or things that could put them in the spotlight; it can cover just about everything. In order for one to stand their ground and to go after their own dreams in life, they will need to feel safe enough to do so.

A Metaphor

For instance, when one is going on a long journey and knows that they must be able to complete the journey, it will be imperative to have a reliable car. Without this one may not make the whole trip or, if they do, it could become a trip that is full of unnecessary problems.

And one's body is very similar to having a car that works: the body, like the car, is the vehicle that one travels through life within. The driver can do what they need to by having a car; without the car, the driver is not going to get very far.

Having a mind is one thing, but without a body, one's experience of life is not going to be too pleasant. This doesn't mean that one has to lose their body in a physical sense, as one can have a body and yet experience life as if they haven't got one.

Connection

Being in the body allows one to experience a life that includes: emotion, connection, pleasure, peace, comfort, and simply being in the present moment. To be in one's head - or above it - can lead to one experiencing the complete opposite of these feelings.

Disconnection

For some people, being out of their body will be how it has been their whole life. Through being like this for so long, one might not even know that this is not how it should be. For others, however, this will be a relatively new occurrence.

Trapped Emotions

To leave the body is normal when it has become too painful to be there. And living in one's head is a natural consequence of an emotional build-up in the body. Another description that is used for trapped emotions is trauma. When emotions are not allowed to be released, they end up staying in the body.

So this could be the result of an experience that was extremely traumatic or an accumulation of experiences that had the same effect. Both one's adult and childhood years could be where the answers to these questions lie.

Adult trauma can be easier to pinpoint, but when it comes to childhood trauma, the mind can forget; the body, though, can never forget. How the body shows this could be confusing, though, and may not be the easiest thing to understand, especially if one's mind has come to the conclusion that these symptoms are normal and how life is.

Awareness

These trapped feelings and emotions will need to be released from one's body in order for them to feel safe there.

Chapter 27

Forgiveness

It is not uncommon for someone to be told that they should just forgive and forget and simply move on from someone who has wronged them. This can seem to be the most logical thing that one can do: to put it behind them and carry on with their life.

One could be told that they are bigger than what has taken place or that holding onto to what has happened will be detrimental to their health and wellbeing. So one might then feel pressured to move on, or at least make other people believe they have moved on to keep them happy.

For others, it could be something that they just go with and don't force themselves to forgive or to go along with what other people expect them to do. It could be a few days or it could be a few weeks, but this doesn't matter, as one will embrace what they are experiencing.

Two Approaches

One can deny how they feel and push the whole experience out of their conscious awareness, or one can embrace what took place and slowly integrate what has happened and move on.

So while one of the examples above is healthy and the other is not, they both give the impression that one has moved on. If one came across two people and each one of them chose one of the options above, it might be hard to tell which one had truly moved on and forgiven, and which one had not.

Another approach is for one to become one with that they are experiencing and to externalize their pain. Here, one is not the observer of what took place, nor is one able to hold what they are feeling; they have become consumed by it.

Violence

This is then likely to lead to some kind of violence towards the person or people who have caused one to feel wronged in some way. And there are going to be actions one can take that are subtle and barely noticeable on one side, to actions that are highly visible on the other.

Just because one is not engaging in external forms of violence, it doesn't mean that no violence is taking place as one could be directing the violence against themselves. So, while the target may be different, the consequences are still the same.

Outlook

What can define how one deals with the need for revenge can be factors such as: whether one is more of an extravert or an introvert, what one's childhood was like, whether one is religious or not, and the kind of people one spends their time with.

The Experience

When the need for revenge arises, it is typically due to someone feeling that they have been harmed or wronged in some way. One could feel that they have been: compromised, betrayed, violated, humiliated, and/or abused, for instance.

And shortly after these feelings arise, one is likely to end up feeling the emotions that are to do with self-protection. Here, one can feel anger and as this builds, hate and rage can appear. These factors can then lead to someone wanting to seek revenge.

Stuck In Anger

It is natural for people to say that they don't want to forgive another and this is often a result of what they believe will happen if they let go of the anger and rage. To do this will leave them wide open to the feelings that are under these emotions and here one will feel vulnerable and without protection.

So to just let go of the anger will not be enough; one will need to face and let go of what is going on at a deeper level in order to feel safe enough to move on. This is why being able to detach is so important, because if one is stuck in how they feel, they will not be able to see that there is another possibility.

Holding on

The mind holding onto anger can cause one to remain stuck in the need for revenge. And this can then result in one holding on to things that happened many, many years ago. To the mind it won't be safe to let go, as this could lead to the same thing happening all over again.

If one feels comfortable enough with their emotions or is around people who encourage them to embrace how they feel, then it is less likely that they will continue to hold on.

Trapped Emotions

So in this case, being angry and seeking revenge is not right or wrong or good or bad; it is simply the result of one protecting oneself. At the time of the wrongdoing, this can be vital to one's survival.

However, if one still feels this way after a certain period of time, it could be a sign of avoidance.

As these deeper feelings and emotions that have become trapped are faced and released from a recent event or an event that happened many years ago, one will be able to let go of one's anger and of the need for revenge. It will no longer be necessary for one to be in this protective mode as they have emotionally moved on from what took place.

To say that one should forgive and forget can sound right, but sometimes, forgiveness is more about what is going on in the body than what is going on in the mind. And therefore, the body needs to be one's focus, and not the mind.

Awareness

If one is still around the people who have wronged them and they have not changed, then it might not be a good idea to let one's guard down. In this case, it might be best to no longer have this person in one's life.

However, when it comes to people one no longer sees, or who do not cause one any problems, it will be important to let go of what has stayed trapped within one's body.

Chapter 28

Grief

After one has certain experiences in their life, they are generally going to feel certain emotions. As we are all emotional beings, this is normal and what is to be expected. But just because this is normal and a part of being human, it doesn't mean that this is what always takes place.

Something can happen in one's life that causes one to end up trying to avoid experiencing the feelings that arose. Therefore, one is not going to fully embrace how they feel and, at some times, one can avoid their feelings completely.

This is something the mind will do as a way to avoid pain and, in this example, it is to avoid emotional pain. After a while, the mind can end up being completely oblivious to the emotions that one has disconnected from in their body.

The body, on the other hand, will be only too aware of this pain; while the mind forgets, the body remembers. It is possible for the mind to believe that the pain has disappeared and no longer exists, but the body will not be so deluded.

Emotional Baggage

What this leads to is what is often described as 'emotional baggage'. Even though emotions are not physical things, they can still end up causing one to feel weighed down, just as one would be if carrying something physical.

147

But it won't just lead to their body feeling heavier, hardened, and burdened; there will be other consequences. Life in general can end up being something that one must endure and not enjoy.

Every other area of one's life can end up paying the price as well, including one's: physical health, relationships, sense of purpose, passion (or lack of it, in this case), and emotional wellbeing.

Stuck

Although the mind can believe that the emotional pain is gone and everything is back to normal, there is a strong chance that it is simply stuck within their body. So instead of moving on from the experiences that caused one to feel as they did, they can end being unable to move on from what has happened.

It is then nothing more than an illusion to say that one has moved on. One might be stuck, numb, and suffer a diminished quality of life, but the mind will still do all it can to avoid facing the pain - the very thing that can lead to one being liberated.

Loss

And one thing that can cause someone to feel emotional pain is when some kind of loss occurs. When one experiences loss, there is also likely to be grief. This can be due to: the loss of a loved one, the loss of a pet, the loss of one's childhood, the end of a relationship, the failure to get one's needs met as a child, and many other things.

Each and every one of us is unique and so not everyone is going to respond in the same way. There is no right or wrong way to respond; how one responds is personal and not something to resist or feel ashamed of.

Grieving

The ideal will be for this grief to be faced and not avoided. However, while this is the best option when it comes to one being able to move on with their life, it doesn't always take place. And this can be due to one feeling uncomfortable with their emotions, as well as being surrounded by people who are similarly uncomfortable.

Possible Reasons

Perhaps one has formed an identity of being strong and emotionless, and if they were to show how they felt, they might lose this image. If this relates to childhood grief, it could be that one's caregivers were out of touch with their own emotions. So one had to deny how they felt, as this is what their caregivers did.

Or if one is around other people who are grieving, one could end up ignoring their own grief. Looking after the people around oneself then becomes the priority and how they feel ends up being ignored. One could be so cut off from their emotions that they don't even realise they are experiencing grief.

In The Body

Time can pass and one can have no awareness of their grief. However, it will be trapped in the body and this can lead to certain consequences. The primary area where it will be held is in one's chest, it will then influence one's: feelings, thoughts, behaviour, and physical body.

This can affect one's posture and cause one to bring their head down and their shoulders in, as a way to protect this area. One can end up withdrawing and have no interest in doing anything new or anything in general. Being depressed can be another consequence of carrying trapped grief.

Physically, it can lead to someone having a nose that never seems to stop running, eyes that water, and having lung problems, amongst others things.

Awareness

In order for one to be present, and to be able to enjoy life, rather than just endure it, it will be important for one to release the grief that has built up in their chest.

As well as the feelings in one's chest, there is also likely to be feelings that are underneath the grief. These will be in the brain that is just above one's stomach, also known as the ego or enteric system. Here, the following feelings could be felt: powerlessness, hopelessness, and death, for instance.

There is no set time for how long this process can take; it can all depend on how much grief one has trapped within their body and how ready one is to let go.

Chapter 29

Illness

In the western world, there is very little attention given to emotions and feelings and the roles that these play in whether the body is in a place of balance or imbalance. The typical approach is to look at things in isolation, and what happens to the body is then a random occurrence.

While we each have a body and a mind, these are often seen as being separate. They are not seen as working together or influencing each other. Through this perspective, the body can be seen as a 'machine' that operates randomly and has no reason for becoming out of balance.

Genetics

At least, this was the case until the trend for genetics was established. Today, the common reason why the body does what is does, is seen as being due to someone's genetics. So while these are perceived as the 'answers', one is nothing more than a sitting duck. One has no real control or influence over what does or doesn't happen to their body: genetics does.

Dead From The Neck Down

And while the west has become incredibly informed at an intellectual level, when it comes to emotions and feelings, it is a completely different story. This then leads to what is often described as being 'dead from the neck down'.

Emotions and feelings have become the casualties of the modern day world. They are often seen as a problem or a distraction and are generally ignored, with very little importance given to them.

Two Realties

The body is where feelings and emotions are found, with the mind producing thoughts and ideas. Life is experienced through the body and yet the mind simply observes what is taking place. So the body is life and the mind has ideas about life. This is often described as duality, with the mind being more passive and body being more active.

The mind is no more important than the body; each aspect plays an important part. One of the biggest challenges in the world today is the disconnection between body and mind. Here, one can live completely in one's head and have no awareness of their body.

Pain

One of the biggest reasons for this is that the body is where not only pleasure, but pain, can be felt. The mind will do all it can to avoid pain; this is simply a matter of survival. So this is not a problem per se, it is completely necessary.

What creates problems is when this approach becomes a way of life, as this will result in one becoming completely cut off from their body. Pain is a part of life and therefore can't be avoided. So what has to take place is the processing of this pain, to stop one from becoming cut off from their body and living solely in their head.

This is something that can take years to occur and is unlikely to happen overnight. But when it does happen, one will not only begin to live in an imbalanced way, they will see life in an imbalanced way.

The Modern Day

Through this, one will no longer experience life through the body and observe life through the mind: one will simply become the observer of life. An internal imbalance has now been formed and this internal imbalance is then projected onto the external world.

Here, the world becomes an example of this imbalance; people are strictly an effect of life, and not a cause; what is going on in one's body is then simply a mystery.

The Mind

The mind has all kinds of defence mechanisms to avoid the body's feelings and emotions, and these are important. If one was to constantly experience these feelings and emotions, it would lead to one being overwhelmed.

But when these feelings and emotions are not processed in some way, the mind will have no other option than to disconnect from them. Not only can one end up being cut off from their feelings and emotions, but they can become alienated from their own body.

Although the mind can then delude itself into thinking these feelings and emotions are no longer there, the body will have something else to say about this.

The Truth

Even though this disconnection has been created, it is not generally recognised in mainstream culture. However, if numerous people are disconnected themselves, there is unlikely to be much opposition to this viewpoint.

So if one lives in their head and is cut off from their body, it will be normal to see things as just happening or being random

And the fact that genetics are commonly seen as being the cause of disharmony in the body is not much of a surprise. The mind is external while the body is internal, and so the mind will see everything as being out there, when in reality this is simply a projection. If it wasn't genetics, then the mind would simply come up with another explanation.

The Body

The ability to listen to the body and to get in touch with one's feelings and emotions will not be there, if one is stuck inside their head. The body's wisdom and answers will go unnoticed; the body could be seen as a lump of meat that goes wrong for no apparent reason (other than one being a victim of one's genetics, for instance) and that what one does has no effect on their body.

But just because the mind is unaware of one's feelings and emotions, it doesn't mean that they have simply disappeared. The body will absorb them and these will end up trapped in ones skin, bones, organs, and muscles, for example.

Invisible Force

And these emotions and feelings can remain hidden and go unnoticed for many years, just as some things in life take time to be built and time to be destroyed. In the short term, everything can seem static, but as time goes by, changes will be noticed and they could be sudden.

These emotions and feelings can have built up due to what has happened in one's adult years and may go right back to when one was a child, a baby, or even in the womb. And these can put a lot of extra pressure and weight on one's body, leaving the body unable to function from a place of harmony as it has been compromised by feelings and emotions.

Awareness

Ideally, there would be a much greater awareness of emotions and feelings in the world, with the mainstream education system educating people on how emotions work and what can happen if they are not dealt with. It would then be normal to be in touch with them and to process them when necessary.

However, at an individual level, one can seek their own answers.

Chapter 30

Inner Child

For people who are interested in self-development, the term 'inner child' may be familiar. Not only might one be familiar with this term, but one may feel very comfortable with it.

When it comes to people who are not into self-development, the whole thing may sound a bit airy-fairy, and be seen as yet another reason for them to avoid going into this area or to do any work on themselves.

While the above could be true, it can also be possible for people interested in self-development to dismiss it, and for people who are not, to embrace the concept. It is not black and white, and will depend on a whole host of factors.

Location

It is generally said that the inner child resides just above the stomach and this is also the area of the ego. Another way to describe this area is to say that it is where one's personal power is to be found. So if one is experiencing challenges when it comes to feeling empowered, this area of their body needs to be looked at.

How stable or unstable one feels emotionally, is also largely defined by what is going on in this part of the body. Recent studies have shown that over ninety percent of serotonin and over fifty percent of dopamine is made in this area.

The Other Brain

To some people this might be a surprise, but if one has a good connection to their body and is reasonably self-aware, it may not be. The fact that one's gut and not the brain in one's head is defining how they feel could be something that they have always sensed or known.

So the inner child, or whatever one wants to call this part of oneself, is in an area of the body that has incredible power over how one feels. And while the ego is often seen as negative or dysfunctional, in many ways the ego is simply an expression of one's inner child.

Inner Child

The inner child will be made up of images, sensations, thoughts, beliefs, and feelings. And even though it is the area above one's stomach where the inner child is thought to reside, it can also be present in other areas of one's body.

So one's chest, lower stomach, hips, and muscles, for instance, can all contain the memories and feelings of one's inner child, but the focal point - in terms of how one feels - is above the stomach.

Experiences

The kinds of experiences that one had as a baby and a child will largely define what one's inner child is like. So there will be two important factors here: how one was treated during these years, and how one interpreted how they were treated.

In astrology, for instance, it is said that one's moon sign represents their inner child. If one is open to this concept, it shows that it is not just one's caregivers that shape what one is like while growing up. It also depends on how one interpreted what happened to one as a child, and this is going be partly influenced by the moon sign one has.

Childhood

But to put one's moon sign to one side, it is clear that the kinds of experiences one had while growing up will have had an impact on the kind of condition one's inner child is in today. Because although one will have physically grown up, their emotional development may have stayed the same and so may still reflect how one felt as a child.

And the child it does reflect is likely to be their inner child. So if one's childhood experiences were generally nurturing and supportive, this inner child could cause very few problems. And yet if one had a childhood which was far from nurturing and supportive, then this inner child is going to continually remind them.

On the other hand, it may be that just one experience was particularly traumatic and left a mark. Something does not have to be overly traumatic to leave a mark; it could be something that simply happened on a regular basis.

Trapped Feelings

Unless someone was around to acknowledge one's childhood feelings and to allow them to be processed, they would have stayed trapped in one's body. So while one physically grew up, their emotional body remained the same.

One could have had experiences that caused them to feel: anger, rage, grief, sadness, abandonment, rejection, powerlessness, hopelessness, trapped, ashamed, guilty, burdened, worthless, and even wanting to die.

Disconnected

Years will have gone by and one could easily have become cut off from these experiences. But even though this is the case, things will happen to make one take notice of what needs to be looked at in their body.

One could find that they overreact to things that happen in their relationships, or that they feel down and depressed for no apparent reason, for example. However, if they were to take the time to tune into this part of themselves, they might find that childhood emotions are calling out to be heard.

Awareness

While the past cannot be changed, it does not mean that the emotional charge of the past can't be removed. The emotional pain that one's inner child is experiencing needs to be faced and released.

As this happens, one's level of emotional development will increase and one will start to let go of their emotional baggage.

Chapter 31

Inner Conflict

When people work together and are on the same side, so much can be achieved. If there is disharmony amongst people, problems can appear and this can lead to things slowing down or stopping completely.

One example that comes to mind here is a sports team. When everyone in the team works together, amazing things can happen. But when just one of the team members is out of alignment with the rest, it can disrupt the team as a whole.

The same thing can apply to someone's life. To have inner conflict can cause all kinds of challenges, and some of these may be so insignificant that they are able to be ignored or overlooked. However, there will be other conflicts that are not possible to push to one side and this is because they are far too impactful to overlook.

Outer Conflict

It is often said that outer conflict is a sign of inner conflict. One can often experience outer struggles and strains as a consequence of what is going on internally, and yet if one is experiencing inner conflict, they often won't have to look as far as that to come to the conclusion that something is not right.

How one feels and thinks, and the emotions that they are experiencing, can cause a lot of inner unease and unrest. This will then mean that how one behaves will reflect what is going on in the inside, and this is unlikely to be functional.

As well as defining how one behaves, inner conflict can define how one sees others and even how one sees the world; there are many different effects that can take place through experiencing inner conflict.

Self-sabotage

One can have the need or desire to have something in their life and yet the opposing forces within stop one from doing what they need. This is often described as self-sabotage, and this is simply another name for inner conflict.

Here, one has a desire to have something and yet doesn't do what they need to do to achieve this. Or, one has attained exactly what it is they wanted and does one thing or a number of things to push it away. To the outsider, this can come across as very strange and not make any sense.

One could be aware of why this is taking place or one may be as baffled as other people are, wondering why they are not going after what they want or why they sabotage exactly what they want.

Examples

There are going to be many areas where this is experienced and the primary areas can be: relationships, success, health, and finances.

One may have the desire to have a loving relationship with another on one level and yet feel incredible fear when another person gets close to them; or one may already be in a relationship that is loving and supportive, and yet because they feel emotionally trapped, end the relationship, resulting in a sense of regret and confusion soon after.

162

The need to grow and express oneself is a natural and healthy need. And while one may desire to learn new skills or improve current skills, there could be feelings that are so powerful that one doesn't learn anything new or allow themselves to progress in life. These could relate to feelings of rejection and abandonment if they were to be seen.

One intention may be to get in better physical shape, by losing or gaining weight. But while this desire is there, there can also be deeper fears that one will feel vulnerable if they lose or gain weight. So, as they don't feel that it is safe, one may not go ahead with their plans or, if they do, one may stop before long.

Inner Harmony

These are just some examples of how inner conflict can affect someone's life, and there are many others. However, while inner conflict can seem normal and how life is, it is not a true reflection of how the body is.

Life is often said to be a journey of letting go and realising that one is already whole and complete. What gets in the way of this is what one picks up over their life. So while some kind of inner conflict could be described as normal, to experience extreme conflict is a clear sign that something is not right.

Emotions And Feelings

To have emotions and feelings that come and go is a part of life, and yet this doesn't always happen. They can end up staying in the body, trapped and therefore hidden from one's awareness. The mind can believe that they no longer exist and that this is the end of it.

But while the mind can live in this delusion, the body pays the price. The body's vital organs, skin, bones, and muscles, will be where they are stored. How one sees life, how one behaves, and the people one attracts and is attracted to, will all be defined by these emotions and feelings.

One may be aware of these from time to time or at certain moments, or may be completely oblivious. When one is aware of them, they will see how their external reality is mirroring them. But if one is not aware, it can appear to be one big mystery.

Parasites

As these trapped feelings and emotions do not belong in the body, they can end up taking over. So instead of one's life being a reflection of what is true for them and what will bring them real fulfilment; it becomes a reflection of these trapped emotions and feelings.

Causes

These could have been trapped in one's body since they were a baby. The experiences one has as an adult can add to these, and yet childhood experiences are often the biggest cause. Growing up in an environment where one's caregivers were physically or emotionally unavailable can be key factors.

One's caregivers would have ignored and dismissed how one felt, and so one would have had no choice but to push their feelings and emotions out of their awareness in order to survive.

Awareness

These emotions and feelings will need to be released from the body. Through this, one can let go of a lot of inner and outer conflict and gradually lead a life that reflects who one really is.

Chapter 32

Intimacy

Although the need to experience intimacy is one of the strongest needs that someone can have, it doesn't mean that this is a need that will always be fulfilled. For some people in the world, intimacy will be part of life and something that is simply taken for granted, having been a part of their life for as long as they can remember.

For others, it will be an experience that seems more or less impossible to achieve. And this is inevitably going to lead to the creation of moderate to extreme pain. Because even though this need is not being met, it won't simply disappear.

The Mind

One thing is for certain here and that is that the mind will come up with all of the reasons under the sun as to why one is not experiencing intimacy; these can range from ideas that sound fairly legitimate to ones that are somewhat farfetched.

Here one can feel like a victim and that they lack what others have. This can include: looks, money, status, intelligence, or some other attribute. One can even come to the conclusion that there is something inherently wrong with them and that they are defective in some way.

If one is not experiencing intimacy, it is not much of a surprise that the mind will form these ideas and perceptions, as the mind observes what is taking place and then labels these occurrences.

Other Factors

As well as what is going on inside one's head, there can also be other influences. But while these can validate what is taking place, they will do little else and can just cause one to stay where they are, not moving on or progressing so as to actually experience intimacy.

These influences can be: friends, family, colleagues, and others. The media can also give reasons and supply its own version of solutions, typically through material consumption. Here, the problem will be seen as solvable though buying different clothes, having the right perfume/aftershave, or in displaying the right jewellery, for instance.

More recently, this has gone on to include changing one's appearance through some kind of surgery, or through gaining the 'perfect' body through the latest craze of endlessly going to the gym. There are also numerous diets one can pursue to supposedly enable one to finally look 'right'.

The Story Maker

To the mind, everything is external and the answers are always available outside. The body, on the other hand, is completely different. While the mind has ideas about life, the body is life. There is no separation when it comes to the body and life.

The mind views life from a place of separation and disconnection. For instance, a travel guide can describe what certain countries are like, but a guide will never match up to the experience of actually travelling those countries. It is simply someone's ideas about the places, and not the places themselves.

So the mind simply assumes and has no real insight into what is going on. The real answers as to why someone is not experiencing intimacy are in the body and not the mind.

The Rejection

However, if one lives in their head and therefore rejects their body, then the body's wisdom and the answers it possesses will be ignored.

While this is often normal in today's world, it doesn't just happen; there is a reason for it and it is typically due to the occurrence of some kind of emotional pain. It could be an experience that was extremely traumatic or it could just as easily be an accumulation of experiences that were painful. By refusing to deal with this pain, one can gradually become stuck in their head.

The mind can use all kinds of different defence mechanisms and escapes to push these emotions outside of one's conscious awareness. But while it is common to avoid these emotions, it can also keep one stuck and therefore unable to move forward in life.

Repression

Just because these emotions have been repressed and may no longer be registered at a conscious level does not mean that they are not having an effect. They can become stuck and frozen in every part of one's body: in the bones, organs, muscles, and skin, for instance.

While the mind may have no recollection of what these emotions are, they will show up in other ways. How emotionally healthy someone is can be known through how functional their relationships are.

Intimacy

So, in order for one to experience intimacy, the body must feel comfortable with it. And if the body is carrying around feelings and emotions from situations in the past where one didn't feel safe, then it is not going to allow intimacy to take place.

The body is simply protecting itself, and part of that process will be to keep people at a distance. The majority of these feelings can come from when one was a child and in how one was treated by their primary caregiver.

Childhood

Here, one could have had a caregiver that was emotionally unavailable, conditional in their love, and unstable, leaving one's childhood needs and wants generally ignored. This can then mean that as a child one was left feeling: invalidated, mismatched, rejected, abandoned, isolated, and even abused in some way.

This figure then became not someone one would have felt safe with, but someone to be feared and kept at a distance. One's sense of trust in people could also have been destroyed through having this kind of caregiver.

The emotions and feelings that one experienced had to be pushed out of one's mind in order to survive, as one's caregivers may have emotionally invalidated them and not regulated their emotions, resulting in these emotions ending up being built up and stored in the body.

Self Made Prison

So during these early years, it was beneficial to keep a distance as it was a matter of survival. But although time has passed, these feelings still exist in the body and as this is what feels familiar, the mind has associated it as what feels safe, so that it is now 'comfortable' to keep people at a distance.

These feelings and emotions can cause one to re-create their reality in a way that mirrors these early experiences. The people that one attracts and is attracted to will be a consequence of these repressed emotions and feelings.

Awareness

These feelings will need to be released from the body and as this takes place, one will be able to feel comfortable with intimacy. As what is going on inside the body changes, what is going on in one's life will change.

Chapter 33

Jealousy

When there is an absence of trust in a relationship certain problems will inevitably arise. Although there are still going to be problems when trust does exist, there is less chance of jealousy appearing and, if it does exist, its effects will be minimal.

As human beings, we have a wide range of emotions that can be experienced. While some of these are regularly classed as positive and some as negative, they are all part of what it means to be human. Some of these can be embraced and some can be denied, but they will always be there and won't just disappear.

Jealousy

Jealousy is an emotion that can't be removed, and yet just because it does appear, it doesn't mean that it reflects reality. It could be the result of what one is projecting onto a certain occurrence or a relationship in general.

When this happens, one is not seeing what is really taking place; one is seeing what they want to see. An interpretation is made and this then becomes the truth, regardless of whether it is actually so.

The Experience

As the emotional experience can be so powerful, it is likely to be a real challenge for one to see when this is the case. This emotion, along with many others, could cause one to lose their ability to be conscious and one could end up doing things that create even more issues.

One's mind can end up being flooded with all kinds of 'negative' thoughts, scenarios, and stories that not only support the way one feels but also have the potential to enhance how one feels.

The Real

During certain moments it is clear that when jealousy does arise, it is for a good reason. It is there to notify someone that something is not right and some kind of action needs to be taken.

If one was in a relationship with another and they displayed behaviours that were inappropriate, one would be unlikely to trust this person and therefore to feel jealous would be normal.

Examples

Perhaps one is with someone who is overly flirtatious and attention-seeking, with the need to gain approval or acceptance from just about every man or woman that they come across.

Boundaries are then a challenge for this person, leaving their partner unsure of what they are going to do with others or what they may allow others to do to them.

The Imagined

When one feels jealous as a result of how they perceive something and not because of how things actually are, the feeling can be taken as truth. Once the mind triggers the emotions, thoughts, and sensations, the ability to see the reality of a situation can disappear.

What they are going through then has nothing to do with what their partner is doing, and has everything to do with their own interpretation of it.

Examples

So one's partner may talk to other men or women, or might decide to go for a night out or to go on holiday without them, leaving one feeling extremely jealous.

Consequences

Uncertainty is then going to consume the mind and this will lead to further consequences. So even though this is just one's imagination and does not reflect reality, one is still going to experience the same things.

One could talk openly about this and deal with it in this way, or one could deal with what is going on for them on the inside. This would be a way to move beyond this challenge in a way that could lead to deeper intimacy and strengthen the relationship.

But if one doesn't talk about it or face what is going on within, the situation could get worse. One could accuse the other person of something that they have not done, potentially creating further distance and perhaps even causing the relationship to end.

A Pattern

It then becomes a self-fulfilling prophecy and although it doesn't reflect the reality of the situation, one's actions will make sure it does. This could be a pattern that one has and this challenge appears over and over again.

So one's current relationship is then fraught with jealousy or one may keep sabotaging their relationships because jealousy completely takes over. One then loses the ability to be objective and to see situations for what they are.

The Trigger

When one experiences jealousy on a regular basis and it has nothing to do with what is taking place, it is going to be due to the ego mind's interpretations. While jealousy can be felt strongly, it is nothing more than a surface level emotion.

For example, one can get angry and this is a way for one to protect oneself against a real or perceived threat. And underneath the anger will be a sense of being compromised or violated in some way and the same applies to jealousy.

A Deeper Look

So below the jealousy is going to be what one feels in their chest and what they feel in their stomach. If one is out of touch with their emotional body, then these may not be easy to identify. Within the chest this could relate to feeling: rejected, abandoned, alone, and a sense of loss, amongst others.

Within the stomach this can relate to: powerlessness, hopelessness, loss of control, and even the experience of death.

Childhood

At first glance, these emotions could seem out of place and extreme and yet they typically relate to one's childhood years. Time has passed and one has grown up physically, but emotionally they have remained the same.

As a baby, one is completely dependent and needs constant attention. To experience a loss of attention as a baby or a child has the potential to cause a lot of emotional pain.

No caregiver is perfect and they don't need to be; there are going to be times when one feels abandoned. This will happen even more when one has been brought up by a caregiver that was neglectful. So, through these emotions and feelings not being dealt with, they would have stayed trapped within one's body.

Awareness

Ideally, when one has a relationship with another adult it is going to be based on trust and mutual choice. Each person is in the relationship because they want to be and not because the other person is forcing them to be.

So if this is the case and one feels jealous, there is a strong chance that their past is still affecting them. To have these trapped feelings and emotions in one's body is going to make it a challenge to respond to life as it is, as opposed to how it once was.

Chapter 34

Letting Go

Life is constantly changing and never stays the same. But while this is the truth about reality, it doesn't mean that letting go and going with the flow of life is necessarily easy or straightforward. The outer world is constantly changing and transforming, and yet the inner world and what is going on within someone can create resistance to this.

And when this happens and there is a resistance to what is taking place, life can become a real challenge. One is then out of alignment, and no longer present and responding to life in real time.

It has been said that the present moment is all there is and that the past and the future are nothing more than an illusion. But when one doesn't let go, they become stuck in the past, or are left thinking about a future that could be better.

The present moment can then end up being lost and wasted as a result. What happened a few weeks ago or even a few years ago can consume one's present moment, which is the only moment where one has a sense of power.

There is no way for one to change what has happened in the past, unless one has a time machine - but at this time, they do not exist and even if they did, to return to the past could lead to further challenges.

Just Let Go

It is not uncommon to hear someone say 'just let go' and while this can sound completely appropriate, it is not always this easy. Just because someone knows that they need to let go intellectually, this does not mean that letting go emotionally is easy.

The intellect is one thing and this responds in a certain way; however, when it comes to one's emotions (or what is often called the emotional body) a completely different approach is often required.

The Body And The Mind

Whereas the mind is more of a doer and does things through force and action, the emotional body does more or less the opposite. To change one's thinking, one must think differently and see differently. That is how the mind is changed and so just 'letting go' is the language of the intellect.

When it comes to the emotional body, using action and force is not how it works. In order to let go and change how one feels, one will need to embrace and be with their emotions. Through this process they will gradually disappear. There is no force or action required; it is a being and not a doing. The words 'just let go' are often seen as a foreign language to the body.

Consequences

One could hear this saying and be at a point in their life where it is possible for them to 'just let go' and all could be well. However, the opposite could also be true and one could end up feeling far worse.

This could cause one to feel weak or that they lack something that others have. They might even end up feeling guilty for holding onto the past and not moving on with their life. The reactions one get can all depend on how emotionally aware the people are who they surround themselves with.

And as emotions are typically overlooked and denied in today's world, avoiding them at all costs is the norm. It is then not so much that 'just letting go' works for people, as much as that it allows them to escape from how they truly feel.

The Battle

One could end up in a battle between their head and body, with the understanding that they should let go and that this is what they need to do on one side, and yet a body that is full of emotions and therefore desperately wants to be heard on the other.

This resistance can be seen as natural due to two possible reasons. If one has been taught that they should just let go, then they won't want to get in touch with how they feel. To do this is going to be seen as a distraction that will simply sabotage their process of letting go.

The other is if one has not developed a healthy relationship to their emotions. If one feels uncomfortable with them, it will feel natural to have very little, if any, connection to them.

Emotional Beings

Each situation one experiences in life causes emotions, and some create more than others. When these emotions are allowed to flow, one will remain in the present. If this doesn't happen, their attention will end up getting caught in the past.

The mind can end up creating thoughts and beliefs based on these feelings, but at the root of it all, it's about the emotional experience that one had. So one has let go of their thoughts or beliefs about what took place, but if the feelings that were caused by what took place have not been released as well, it won't make much difference.

Trapped Emotions

A clear example of this is when one experiences some kind of traumatic event or an accumulation of minor events that are equally traumatic. When trauma is experienced, one does not go through the complete emotional experience, and so one ends up staying stuck in a feeling cycle that was unable to be completed.

One can then end up losing touch with these feelings in order to protect oneself and can end up living in their head as a result. This is done for protection and is not something that one should feel ashamed of doing.

All the time these emotions and feelings are trapped in one's body, one's attention is going to be brought back to the past in some way; it is the emotional charge that causes one to do this.

Awareness

Once these trapped feelings and emotions have been released, the emotional charge of the event will go and letting go will be a natural consequence.

Chapter 35

Loss

This is something that can affect someone in many ways and as a result of many things. Some losses can simply be ignored and forgotten about, while others are harder to forget.

One can also lose something and never forget the loss, regardless of how much time goes by or what else may happen in their life. What will often define the impact of the loss is how emotionally attached one was.

To lose a loved one can often be one of the most challenging losses that one can experience. And yet, as people, we can become attached to almost anything, meaning that loss is a subjective experience and a part of life.

One loss cannot be compared to another and neither should it be. If one has experienced a loss and feels a certain way, it must be acknowledged. It shouldn't be a question of whether it is an appropriate reaction, or of how it compares with what others are going through or have gone through.

With loss comes grief, and this is something that can't be forced or rushed; it is a process that has to be allowed to take place and for however long it takes.

Examples

Above I mentioned that the loss of a loved one is one of the most painful losses one can experience. And what can also be painful is the loss that one experiences when: a pet dies, a relationship ends, or a job finishes, for example.

There are also losses that have very little impact; one may lose a piece of their clothing or even their car keys. In comparison, these may seem insignificant and even irrelevant.

One of the reasons that these losses don't always register is due to one not being emotionally attached to these things; the first examples are often what one is extremely attached to.

Loss

It is often said that loss has more impact than gain does. So as good as gaining something may be, human beings would rather avoid a loss than experience a gain.

One reason for this is that when humans were living in caves and killing animals with spears, it was most important that they had enough food. To have more was not important, as long as they had enough. To lose what they had would likely have led to starvation and resulted in death.

The Ego Mind

However - regardless of whether the above is true or not - the way the ego mind functions can explain a lot. The ego's main priority is to keep things the same, and what is familiar is classed as what is safe to the mind.

This means that all change is therefore interpreted as death to the mind. And as this is the case, when something comes to an end it will then lead to one having an experience of death. Death is then not something that one experiences once in their life, but many times.

Change

As the ego mind works this way, it means that loss is a part of life and cannot be avoided. The reason for this is that change can't be avoided; this becomes more of a challenge due to the ego mind's interpretation of loss as death.

And while some losses lead to intense grief, others will lead to minimal grief. For losses that really impact one's life, grief could last for many years and even a lifetime. For minimal losses that may not even be noticed, it may be possible to process the loss in a matter of moments and without one being consciously aware of it.

Attachment

As human beings, we become attached to things and this attachment can lead to both pleasure and pain. When it comes to a relationship, for example, some kind of attachment is inevitable.

One can know that the more one gets attached to something, the greater the loss can be. Yet, due to the benefits, it is often a risk worth taking in life.

What can lead to a greater sense of loss when something comes to an end is when unprocessed losses from the past are triggered. The current loss will then be added to a history of unprocessed losses; this may well become overwhelming and hard to handle.

The Past

Just because one has experienced a loss and therefore needs to grieve, it doesn't mean that this will always take place. This will depend on many factors and one of the most significant will be whether one feels safe enough to do so.

These could be losses that one has experienced as an adult and losses that one experienced as a child. One might remember the adult losses, but have forgotten about the losses of their childhood.

Awareness

No matter where these losses have come from or how strong they are, it is important that one allows oneself to grieve them. Although one won't necessarily be able to forget what happened, it doesn't mean that one has to carry the pain around with them forever.

Chapter 36

Manifestation

When it comes to what one attracts and doesn't attract into their life, thoughts are often the primary focus. When someone has this point of view, they are seen as the key to one attracting what they want and repelling what they don't want.

So here, one needs to become hypervigilant when it comes to their thoughts, and to constantly create thoughts that are 'positive'. Through this process, it is said that one will create feelings that reflect their thought processes.

This then creates the impression that the mind is in control of what one feels or doesn't feel. And that how one feels is always a consequence of what one is thinking. Communication is therefore only occurring one way, from the head down and not from the body up.

If one has feelings that are not related to what they are thinking about, then that is said to be due to them having thoughts that they are not aware of. And as their awareness increases, they will be able to notice these thoughts and therefore be able to stop themselves from having these feelings.

The Head

This creates the impression that one's point of focus needs to be on what is going on in their head. And through placing one's attention on this part, one will gradually begin to master their personal reality.

Thoughts are then incredibly important and one will need to become almost obsessed with what they are thinking or not thinking. To

187

ignore them could lead to minor problems and what could be described as major calamities.

Alongside thoughts are one's beliefs, and these are often said to create the thoughts that one has and, therefore, their feelings. These exist in one's mind also, but not in one's conscious mind but their unconscious mind.

The Body

What this would mean is that the body is simply an effect of what is taking place in one's head. The head is the master and the body is the servant. If this is true and the body is nothing more than a lump of meat that is being controlled by what is going on in the head, then it is irrelevant.

To ignore what is going on in one's body and to place one's awareness firmly in their head would be the obvious thing to do. And based on conventional wisdom, why would one think any differently?

The problem here is that conventional wisdom is not always accurate and just because one wants something to be true and 'believes' that is it, it does not mean that it is.

Feelings

What is often heard when it comes to creating one's life, is that one's thoughts create their feelings. What this misses out is the fact what while thoughts can create how one feels, they can also work the other way round.

So how one thinks is a result of how one is feeling, and thoughts are needed to create these feelings in the first place. The reason for this is that feelings exist in the body and the mind then interprets these feelings and produces thoughts and beliefs.

These feelings are what create the resonance that defines what one attracts into their life and what they repel. The thoughts that one has are generally nothing more than a reflection of how one feels and are rarely the other way around.

Trapped Emotions

The feelings and emotions that are in one's body could have been there since one was a baby. They could be the result of what has happened during one's adult years, but it is what takes place in the beginning of one's life that often has the biggest impact on one's reality.

In these moments, one could have had an experience that was extremely traumatic or accumulation of minor experiences that built up and had the same effect over time. These can include the following feelings: hopelessness, powerlessness, worthlessness, helplessness, shame, guilt, and fear, amongst others.

If these emotions and feelings were mirrored and allowed to be released, they would disappear. But when this doesn't happen, they end up being trapped in one's body.

Attraction

Time will pass and the intellectual brain in one's head will become conditioned and 'educated' by society and one is likely to lose all connection to what is going on in their body. But even though one can have no awareness of the feelings and emotions within their body, it doesn't mean that they are not having an effect on one's life.

These trapped feelings and emotions will define what one attracts into their life and what they repel. So the people they are attracted to and the people they attract will all reflect what is going on in their body.

Consequences

When one is cut off from their body and primarily operates from their head, it will be normal for one to come to the conclusion that life is just happening to them, and that they are simply observing what is or is not showing up.

This is part of the duality: the mind observes life and the body experiences life. As the same feelings and emotions are trapped in one's body, one is going to create the same reality. If one is on reverse, they won't go forward unless they change gear.

Breaking The Pattern

In order for one to break the patterns in their life and to create a new reality, it will be essential for them to release these trapped feelings and emotions. When they are not released, the same reality will appear and this will just validate the beliefs and thoughts that the mind has.

Feelings and emotions that are created from the new experiences in one's life will pile on top of one's original feelings.

Awareness

What can make this such a challenge is that one has to detach from what is showing up in their life and what is taking place within them; to react to it will only cause one to be a slave and to remain stuck. It is also important to realise that life is impersonal; it is responding to what one is resonating.

And when things are not going to plan or when one is attracting what they don't want, it is natural to get angry and frustrated. But to remain this way in the long term won't lead to progress. The mind will feel validated and yet what is showing up is a result of what is going on within one's body.

As these emotions are released, one's reality will change and their thoughts and beliefs will follow suit.

Chapter 37

Neediness

To have needs is part of being human and this is something that cannot be changed. One might pretend that they don't have any and yet this is nothing more than a facade and an act of self-denial.

There can also be people who come across as extremely needy, leaving no confusion as to whether this person has needs or not. This is not to say that some people always cover up their needs and others will show them in full, as each person can change depending on the context.

The other dynamic here is when someone has needs and they embrace them for what they are. This means they are nether needy or needless and are comfortable with the fact that they have these feelings.

Disconnected

So when someone has lost all contact with their needs or has very little connection to them, this is not much chance they will ever be met. For one thing, one doesn't know what they are, and if one doesn't know what they are, how could anyone else have any idea either?

This is going to lead to a sense of frustration and pain, and one is likely to end up feeling powerless. And it is then not so much that other people are not responding to their needs, as much as they are out of touch with them themselves.

There could also be moments when this person does come into contact with their needs and they end up feeling incredibly needy as a result. But before long, they are soon disconnecting once more and putting on the mask of being needless.

Never Enough

In the case where someone is needy, it won't matter whether one is getting their needs met or if they are not; as the same consequences are likely to arise. This is because these are not like normal needs that can be met and fulfilled.

These are needs that are insatiable and are unable to be fulfilled in most cases. However, if one has become completely consumed by them and is enslaved to them, one is unlikely to see that they are running on a wheel that never stops.

Just like the person who is generally unaware of their needs, this person could also have moments where they deny them. This will take place on very rare occasions or moments, though.

Comfortable

To be comfortable with one's needs, and not feel overly needy or attached to getting them met, shows that this person is likely to have slightly different needs to the needs of the people above. They could be described as adult needs and these needs can be met and fulfilled by both other people and by themselves.

Attachment

Through not being overly attached to getting one's needs met and being able to have one's needs fulfilled, support is likely to be available in one way or another. When one is attached to getting their needs met either consciously or unconsciously, it often makes it harder to have them met.

One can then become more attached and then it becomes even harder. The cycle then continues and one can end up feeling trapped and overwhelmed by their needs. Being attached ends up pushing what one wants even further away.

The Difference

Being overly needy or needless are two sides of the same coin and being comfortable with one's needs and being neither needy nor needless is often a sign of emotional maturity. So while each person is physically an adult, they do not come from the same place emotionally.

It is not that some people are simply able to have their needs fulfilled in life and that some are not; what it comes down to is how attached someone is and what these needs actually are. Physical growth is something that occurs whether one puts any effort in or not, and yet emotional growth rarely just happens. This is something that can take a conscious effort and a prolonged commitment.

Childhood Needs

The needs of a child or baby are insatiable and need to be met during the right moments. While one may have physically grown up, at an emotional level one can still feel as they did during these early years. One then feels like a child in an adult's body, but if they are not aware of this, they can expect other people to fulfil these needs.

This, however, is not going to be possible, as other people have their own needs and can't be expected to fulfil the needs that one's caregiver didn't meet when they were younger.

195

Trapped Emotions

So when these needs were not met by one's caregiver, this would have created emotional pain and this would have stayed trapped in one's body. Perhaps one's caregiver was emotionally unavailable and out of tune with one's needs, and so one had to go without getting them met in the majority of cases.

As they were emotionally unaware, they couldn't mirror or validate how one felt and so one had no other choice but to repress how they felt. Time has then passed, but emotionally, it can feel as though nothing has changed.

Awareness

These trapped feelings and emotions will need to be gradually released from one's body. As this takes place, one will see that they were not real needs to begin with and that no one could ever fulfil them. Ultimately one is grieving what didn't happen in their childhood, and as a result of this release, one will begin to feel like an adult.

Chapter 38

Negative People

What is clear that is that life is not always a bed of roses: there are ups and downs, and sometimes there can be more downs than ups. For some people, there may be more ups than there are downs, but for others, downs may outweigh the ups.

One might then come to the conclusion that some people are luckier or more fortunate than others. When this opinion is based purely on what is happening externally, it can seem accurate and true.

However, if one was to look within someone and see what is taking place there, they might soon see that there is a reason why they are experiencing more ups than downs, or why they are able to see life in a positive light even though life hasn't always gone their way.

Different Types

Life is made up of different types of people and some people can come across as always being positive and happy, while others can come across as always being negative and unhappy.

There will also be people who swing between the two and who don't seem to stay fixed in either option for very long. But whether one feels positive or negative, this will be the result of a combination of what is happening externally and what is happening internally.

The Mind

In the external world, certain things can take place that cause one to feel positive, and at other times, things can happen that make one feel negative. But while the external world can play a big part in how one thinks and feels, so can their mind.

What takes place externally is interpreted by the mind and the interpretation that is made will play a part in one's thoughts and feelings. It also works the other way too, with one's thoughts and feelings impacting what happens to them externally.

Extremes

Being positive all of the time may be seen as being better than always being negative, and yet there are going to be downsides to this. One might be admired by some, but end up labelled as being in denial by others.

And as life is not always pleasant, one would have to be in denial to always be positive. The mind works in polarities, and so as a way to avoid pain, it can end up going to the opposite extreme. Therefore, one can end up needing to be happy and positive all the time as a way to avoid how they truly feel.

Based on this, being ceaselessly positive or negative are simply two sides of the same coin. One person is simply embracing how they feel and think and what is taking place externally, and another is doing all they can to avoid what is taking place.

Survival

When it comes to one's survival as a human being, focusing on what is negative is more important than focusing on what is positive. Placing one's attention on what makes them feel good might be pleasurable, but it is not necessarily going to ensure their survival.

Whereas if one pays attention to what is negative and therefore what is or what could be a threat to their survival, they are more likely to avoid it and stay alive. This ability is surely one of the reasons why human beings have survived for as long as we have.

So, it is in the interest of one's survival to focus on what is negative. However, it is easy for one to place their attention on what is negative, even when their survival is not under threat. As what we focus on grows, it is important to monitor the mind's tendency to focus on what is negative.

Stuck

If one's attention if placed completely on what is negative and one is unable to see life in any other way, this can be a sign that they are emotionally stuck. This is the world of duality and while there are 'bad' things, there are also 'good' things.

And while one can end up always being positive as a way to avoid facing how they feel, they can also end up always being negative due to not consciously facing how they feel. So whether one is always positive or negative, they are still being controlled by their trapped feelings.

Consequences

These will then define how one thinks and behaves, as well as define one's perceptions, and this will then end up influencing one's reality. The people they attract into their life and are attracted to, as well as the situations they find themselves in, will also reflect how they feel.

How one feels shapes their outer world, and then the outer world ends up influencing how one feels on the inside. It also works the other way around, with one's external reality affecting their inner world.

If one is already full of negativity, it won't take much to put them into a negative state – that's if they are not already in one. If one is fairly neutral within, however, there is going to be less chance of what is happening externally to have an impact on how one feels.

Trapped Emotions

When one has trapped emotions in their body, it is going to be a challenge for them to experience life in a way that is not negative. These feelings will influence both their inner and outer world, so it can be hard for them to detach from what is happening and to see that they have become trapped in a cycle.

The following emotions can be trapped in one's body: grief, shame, powerlessness, hopelessness, rejection, abandonment, and guilt, amongst others.

Awareness

As these are released, one will feel different and therefore their thoughts and behaviour will change; this inner change will gradually have an impact on one's outer reality.

Chapter 39

Negative Thoughts

The term 'negative thoughts' has become very well-known in today's world; this is true for people who are interested in self-development and for those who are not. Thoughts are generally the primary focus in the area of change and personal transformation.

These are said to control how one behaves, what they achieve or don't achieve, and even create reality itself. So if someone deals with their thoughts, their whole life can change. This can range from removing thoughts, to replacing them with so-called 'positive thoughts', and simply just being with them.

The mind's thoughts are primary, and the emotions and feelings of the body are often secondary. According to this concept, if one removes their thoughts, then one's feelings and emotions will also be dealt with. This is the general outlook, and so feelings and emotions can end up being overlooked.

Conventional Wisdom

And when something has been around for a long time or is believed by enough people, it can become known as the absolute truth. But just because something is seen as the truth, it doesn't mean that it is actually true.

Thoughts are often labelled as being the main problems and as what need to change in order for one to live a better life or to experience inner peace. While this can sound right and appear to be the truth, there is a lot more to it.

The Reflection

Although one can be disconnected from their body and therefore their feelings and emotions, it doesn't mean that the mind will be unaffected. The mind will have to respond in some way to what is going on in one's body.

The approach the mind takes will typically depend on what is going on in the body and on how strong the emotional pain is. If one is experiencing strong emotions in their body, then the mind will have to utilise certain defence mechanisms to try to settle everything down.

Defence mechanisms are not negative or bad; they are simply used to stop the mind from being overwhelmed by the pain that is coming up from the body. So when there is emotional pain in the body, the mind can be kept busy.

Obsession

One of the ways it can deal with what is going on in the body is to become obsessive. Here, the mind will produce all kinds of thoughts and ideas to avoid the body's feelings and emotions.

Interpretations

As the mind is the observer of life, it comes to understand life and the body through interpretation. The body, on the other hand, is life and is experiencing everything firsthand. So when feelings and emotions appear in the body, the mind will interpret them in a certain way.

This is similar to what happens when one engages in intellectualisation and this means that one is not feeling their feelings and emotions. The mind is trying to understand them and make sense of them. This is done to avoid facing them, due to the pain that would be created if one did.

Feelings And Emotions

The feelings and emotions in the body that the mind is trying to understand through interpretation can include: rejection, abandonment, fear, grief, loss, betrayal, shame, guilt, powerlessness, hopelessness, and many others.

These emotions could be the result of what has happened during one's adult years, but could also be a consequence of what happened when one was: a child, a baby, or in the womb. Although times have changed, they have remained trapped in one's body.

The Disconnection

If one was aware of their body and what is going on in there, they would be able to see that their thoughts are often nothing more than a reflection of how they feel. So through interpretation, the mind will create all kinds of thoughts as a result of a feeling (or cluster of feelings) that arises.

Examples

When feelings come up in the body, there is the potential for all kinds of thoughts to follow. This is because the mind can interpret things in so many ways and so as to mean many different things.

Abandonment And Rejection

Feelings of abandonment and rejection could appear in the body after the end of a relationship and the mind can then interpret that to mean that: one is unworthy of love, others don't like them, they will always be alone, other people are more attractive than they are, they are a failure, their body is not the right shape, and they may never be in another relationship again, for instance.

Shame

One could feel shame within and this could lead to the following interpretations being made by the mind: that one stands out and doesn't belong, that other people have something they don't have, that they are unworthy of experiencing good things, that other people look down on them and don't like them, that they don't deserve to exist, that one is useless, and many others.

Letting Go

Based on how one feels, these interpolations that the mind has made can seem completely accurate. However, if these feelings were not in the body, the mind would have nothing to interpret.

As these feelings and emotions are released from the body, the mind will be able to settle down.

It is often said that if one changes their thoughts they will change their life. Perhaps a more appropriate saying would be – if you let go of your trapped feeling and emotions, your life will change.

Chapter 40

Painful Memories

While one can form memories that are pleasurable and remind them of moments that were special and uplifting, it is also possible for one to hold onto memories that are painful, reminding them of moments that were stressful and even traumatic.

This is a part of life and there is unlikely to be anyone on the planet who has memories that are only pleasurable or neutral; that is unless one is emotionally numb and therefore can't feel pleasure or pain.

But with that aside, if one was to only have good experiences, they would soon lose their impact. One would no longer have the experiences that were 'bad' to create a sense of perspective in their life. It is the bad experiences that allow one to have a greater appreciation of the 'good' experiences.

So as life is not perfect and consists of experiences that are not always uplifting, one will have memories that they would rather not have. Having these memories is not a problem per se; the problem is when these memories remain emotionally charged.

Painful Experiences

When something painful happens, one is going to have a certain emotional experience. This will be partially based upon what actually happens, and partially based upon one's interpretation of what happens. If one allows themselves to process the feelings that arise, the memory will lose its charge over time.

However, if one's emotional experience is not processed and their feelings get pushed out of their awareness, the memory's emotional charge will remain. This is unlikely to be something that happens consciously; it could just happen naturally.

Protection

The mind will use different defence mechanisms to protect one from the emotional pain that arises. The emotions will then stay in one's body and the mind can become disconnected from them.

One reason this pain becomes pushed out of one's awareness is because it is too overwhelming for them to handle. This is then the only option available and the one action that allows them to handle what happened.

Support

It could be that there was no support around or if there were people around, perhaps it wasn't acceptable for them to reveal what they were going through. The conclusion was made that is wasn't safe for one to embrace their feelings.

If, on the other hand, the people around them were supportive, what can still get in the way is if one doesn't feel comfortable with their emotions. It then won't matter who is around, as one will stop themselves from allowing their emotions to come to the surface.

Causes

Painful memories can be the result of one having experiences that were extremely traumatic and shook one to their very core. This could relate to: abuse as a child and/or as an adult; a car accident; the loss of a family member, pet or friend; the ending of a relationship; or a job loss, for example.

As each and every one of us is different, it means that not everyone is going to react in the same way. One person could experience a loss or have a certain experience without too much trouble, whereas if this were to happen to another person, it could have a far greater impact.

Different Reasons

This could be due to one person being more emotionally stable than another, for instance. How nurturing their childhood was can also have an effect on how emotionally resilient they are and can therefore influence how they respond to experiences.

If one is carrying emotional pain form their childhood or from a later experience that was painful, this could make it harder for them to cope with what happens to them.

Emotional Experience

But no matter what has happened in the past, in order for one to take charge of how they feel and not allow their memories to take control, they will need to process their feelings. If they are left and not dealt with, one will continue to be haunted by what happened - no matter how long ago the experience was.

When the experience occurred, it may not have been possible to face how one felt. And even though time has passed, one might still find it difficult to face how they feel; one could be in touch with how they feel, or they could have become numb.

Assistance

This is why it is important for one to reach out and to get the assistance that they need. To try and face one's feelings by oneself could be overwhelming. So it would be no surprise if one has done all they can to avoid them. This doesn't mean that one is weak or lacks courage; it is simply the result of their mind doing what it can to stop one from being overwhelmed.

Awareness

The kind of assistance that one needs can depend on how emotionally charged one's memories are.

However, the most important thing is that one reaches out for help and doesn't allow their past to control their life any longer.

Chapter 41

Physical Pain

When one experiences some kind of physical pain or tension, it can be normal to see it only as the body reacting to something: that some kind of external solution is needed to deal with the pain, and that the pain simply needs to be removed or numbed to return everything, generally, back to normal.

And this is a natural consequence of seeing the body as separate from the mind and as something that often acts in strange and unexpected ways, ways that will be forever outside of one's intellectual grasp.

Options

There are all kind of options available now to remove this pain, from tablets to patches, drinks, and certain kinds of exercise, for instance. Sometimes these methods will last for a short time and others will last longer.

Perhaps one can remove their pain completely through doing this; it can all depend on many factors. It could also be possible to remove one kind of pain but find, as time goes on, that another kind will appear somewhere else. This time it could be a lot stronger, and it may no longer be possible to remove this pain through the usual means.

Avoidance

As it is human nature to avoid pain and seek pleasure, it is not much of a surprise to see this approach mirrored in the western world. In other societies - in the east, for instance - a different approach is often taken.

So as soon as physical pain appears, one does all they can to put it to an end. One then returns to their normal level of comfort or even feels slightly better. This then enables them (in most cases) to return to their life without bodily discomfort.

Health Care

When one goes to their doctor or to a pharmacy to seek assistance for physical pain, they are not necessarily asked about what else is going on for them. The pain is typically going to be viewed in isolation and not as a single part of something more.

So the experience one has had at an emotional level up until this point will not be explored; it will generally be overlooked. One might be asked what they have been doing physically or what they have eaten recently, but very little else.

The perspective that the body is separate from the mind and therefore acts however it wants is supported by just about every area of the western world. In recent years, genetics has taken over as the chief reason as to why the body does the things it does.

Powerless

There is then the question of what someone has eaten, or if they have done something that was physically strenuous, for example; there is also the genetic component, but other than that, there is very little else. Therefore it would be normal and even expected for one to end up feeling powerless, and that they had no control over their body.

One is then nothing more than an observer of their body and what it does or does not do. And when one lives in their head and is cut off from their body, there is not much chance of another point of view. Of course, one could read about their body being part of who they are, but this is merely an intellectual understanding.

Emotional Disconnection

When someone has a friend that causes them too much pain or when there is a certain place that causes painful memories, it is common to no longer see this person or go to the place. This is done to protect oneself from pain, and as this person and place is not part of oneself; they can be cut out of one's life.

The same approach can be utilised when it comes to emotional pain. Here, one becomes cut off from their body as a way to avoid pain. But while people or places can be removed from one's life, the body cannot be. This will always be there, regardless of whether one has removed their awareness from it.

To the mind, this emotional pain could no longer be there, just like the friend who one doesn't see or the place one no longer goes to. So the mind can live in this delusion and yet the body still carries these emotions and feelings.

Trapped Emotions

These could have built up from what has happened during one's adult years and what took place when they were a child and a baby. Over the years, they can become pushed into one's vital organs, muscles, and bones, and while one may no longer be in touch with them, they will appear in other ways.

And one way they can show up is through one experiencing some kind of physical pain or tension. Through one being cut off from one's emotions and feelings for so long, when this does start showing up as pain it can be confusing. This is partly due to the time delay and also due to the fact that it can take a while for emotional pain to change into physical pain.

Triggers

So one could experience something or even eat something, and these trapped emotions and feelings will be triggered once more and physical pain will ensue. This is because the body wants to release these emotions and feelings to restore inner balance and harmony.

However, if one is taking tablets or something similar to remove the pain, they are also missing out on what the body is trying to communicate. And this information can be far more profound than the fact that the body is in pain.

Areas Of The Body

Different areas of the body can carry different feelings and emotions. The chest can relate to the following feelings: rejection, abandonment, grief, betrayal, emptiness, and hopelessness. In the stomach area it can be to do with: fear, powerlessness, control, shame, guilt, and feelings to do with survival.

These are just some areas and there are others that can carry different feelings and emotions. What is going on within these vital organs can define how one's legs and arms feel, such as feeling cold. Having this emotional build-up causes strain on one's organs and this can impact the body's equilibrium.

Chapter 42

Rage

It has recently been reported that rage could be the result of what is going on for someone at a biological level. While this has been said, figures have also questioned if it is the other way around, with rage causing one's biology to change and not one's biology causing rage.

However, whether one is an expert or an amateur when it comes to biology, it is not going to be much of a surprise to hear that when one feels a certain way, the physical body is also mirroring the experience.

But to say that one's biology is causing one to feel rage or any other emotion, means that one is nothing more than a passive observer: that they have no control and are therefore not responsible for how they feel or don't feel.

To look at it this way would mean that drugs would be one of the few options. This would treat the 'machine' and put at end, at least momentarily, to what the body is doing. Based on this outlook, the mind and the body are separate and both are doing their own thing.

The Old Way

So if rage is a problem for someone, they could end up becoming dependent on drugs or another outside source. And if one has struggled with this for most of their life, this might sound like the only solution available.

The need to go deeper is then taken away and all because someone out there is giving them the 'answers' they need. This is like the parent that does everything they can for their child; the child may enjoy it, but it keeps them in a regressed state of being.

They are unable to grow up and realise who they are. In this example, the parent gets a sense of power and control. But when it comes to the drug companies, not only do they experience power and control over people, but they also receive money and lots of it.

Arrested

This is not to say that drug companies as a whole and everyone who works for them are hell-bent on keeping people in a dependent and powerless state. But this is one of the consequences that arises from telling people that they have very little, if any, control over what is going on with them.

Fortunately, this is a time where people are beginning to realise their power and are no longer willing to give it away, moving from a dependent and powerless state of being to their true state of empowerment and interdependence.

Three

In the western world, there is a complete focus on what is going on in one's physical body. And this has gradually gone on to include what is going on in one's mental body. What hasn't yet been included is one's emotional body and this means that a lot of valuable information is going unnoticed.

One way to lose touch with this body is through being stuck in one's head. And this generally happens as a result of pain building up in the body; living in one's head is then what feels safe. From this position, one's physical body is separate and one has no control over it.

This then comes down to the same reason, with it being likely that one has left their body because it was too painful and now can't get back into their body because of the pain they will experience.

The Mystery

So as one has left their body, it is not much of a surprise that they don't understand why they feel as they do or what is going on there. It's a bit like standing by a swimming pool and wondering what it would be like to experience it.

It would be obvious that one needs to get into the pool in order to understand what it is like, and the same thing applies to understanding oneself. One needs to get back into the body and as they do this, answers will start to appear.

When one is not in the water, they are going to rely on the people who are in there to tell them what it is like. And sometimes these people will be honest, but at other times they will say things that are inaccurate or that only reflect what they are going through.

To be out of one's body means that one will look outside for the answers and these might be right, but they could also end up being completely false.

Rage

To experience rage could make one feel out of control and all kinds of damage could ensue as a result. One's relationships and health could suffer, as well as one's career. This could be something one experiences on a regular basis or on the odd occasion.

Being around others may not be necessary for one to feel rage, as they could be by themselves, with their thinking alone enough to trigger it. Rage is similar to anger; the difference being that it is far stronger and is more of a whole-body experience. It is not just a feeling; one can end up being possessed by it and lose all control.

Stuck

One can then end up stuck in the rage and after a while, return to how they were. They could feel guilty and ashamed for what they have done or feel that they were justified in how they reacted. But as this all happens so fast, they might not even be aware of why they became filled with rage in the first place.

However, while one can be out of touch with their full emotional spectrum, they can still be in touch with things like: anger, rage, irritation, and hate. These emotions appear when one feels threatened in some way and that their survival may be at risk.

Under The Rage

So experiencing rage or any of the other emotions mentioned above is going to give a sense of violation and compromise; what the rage does is allow one to avoid feeling these deeper emotions.

To feel them would cause one to feel vulnerable and to feel rage allows them to feel safe and protected.

Causes

One may have had one experience or numerous experiences where they felt violated recently or many years ago, the anger from that moment or moments staying inside them and building until they became rage. This could go back to when one was a child or baby and could be the result of some kind of abuse or neglect.

But because it was so long ago, one has lost touch with what actually happened. What they haven't lost touch with is how angry it made them feel.

Awareness

So time has passed and yet emotional experiences of the past have stayed trapped in the body. Whenever one gets into a situation that reminds them of it, everything gets triggered and one overreacts.

It will be important for one to release the emotional experience from their body, meaning that they will then have no reason to feel rage. They will be able to be present, instead of projecting their past onto the present.

Chapter 43

Reactive Behaviour

We all have our own style of behaviour and this can change when one is around different people and based on how one feels. One's growth and changes as a person can also lead to one's behaviour altering.

There will be times when one's behaviour is a response to situations and other times when it is a reaction. If it is a response, it will be coming from a place of awareness and self-control. If it is a reaction, it will be coming from a place of unawareness and lack of self-control.

Part Of Life

There are always likely to be times when one reacts in life. Yet if this has become something that takes over one's life, it will create problems.

It may be something that affects one's relationships with friends, family, colleagues, and one's intimate relationships. If one has children – or even pets – they may also end up in the crossfire.

Overreaction

Overreaction is often described as something that should be low on the scale and ends up being high up the scale. This could be overreacting in a way that is an eight, when in reality it was only a two, for example.

To others, it is clear that one is overreacting and behaving disproportionately. However, unless one is aware of this, one will continue to do the same things.

Consequences

What this kind of behaviour can lead to and create are extreme consequences. Emotionally this could be to do with aggression, rage, and showing heightened levels of anger. It can also affect the other side of things and include: sadness, rejection, guilt, anxiety, grief, shame, and hysteria.
The first examples are emotions that usually get projected outwards, while the second examples are emotions that usually become interjected. Although they are different, they can both create reactive behaviour.

Reactive behaviour is created through one acting on these emotions. This means that other people are exposed to these emotions as a result of them building up. If it wasn't for the reactive behaviour, other people may not even know that such strong emotions exist within the person.

Short-term Solutions

It is also possible for people to manage these emotions in a way that leads to short-term solutions, therefore minimising the reactive behaviour. Certain rituals and habits then alleviate the emotions, like a pressure valve. But this won't last for long and would need to be constantly undertaken.

A Closer Look

If one's behaviour to others seems completely out of proportion, it means that something within the individual is out of sync. Based on the individual's interpretations of what they are experiencing, their reaction seems appropriate.

There may even be times when one looks back and cannot understand why they did what they did. There will always be others, however, who can't see anything wrong with how they reacted. It will all depend on how aware the person is.

Interpretations

The ego mind interprets things based on the associations that it has formed. This means that how something is interpreted is subjective, and will be the result of everything one has experienced up until this point.

While to one person, certain behaviour may be seen as an overreaction, another person might interpret it as the right and only way to behave, based on one's ego mind's associations of the experience.

The challenge is that interpretations made by the ego mind's associations may be completely wrong; this is what leads to reactive behaviour.

The Trigger

Once the experience has been interpreted by the ego mind to match these associations, it triggers the emotions and this provides fuel for the behaviour. But these emotions do not just emerge once and then end; the same occurrences appear again and again.

Whether these emotions are released or not, they will always be bubbling under the surface, ready to rise at any moment; a weed can be cut off, but it will soon grow back.

Repression

These are typically emotions that have been repressed for long periods of time, and will not simply disappear. They need to be expressed in some way, and the body is constantly pushing them to the surface, looking to release them.

This means that the ego mind will constantly be looking for situations that will allow for such a release to occur, otherwise it will simply interpret situations in such a way that will lead to a release.

Causes

Traumatic experiences of one's adult life can be a factor here, as can traumatic experiences of childhood. No matter what created these situations or when they occurred, the body will naturally wish to release the feelings resulting from them.

However, the ego mind will seek to avoid these feelings at all costs and will do all it can to distance itself from them. All kinds of defence mechanisms can be used to do this. This is not a bad or negative characteristic, per se: it is simply what the ego mind does to ensure survival.

Survival

From the point of view that the ego mind's main function is to keep one alive, this attribute is a wonderful thing. The problem is that although the mind may have pushed these feelings out of conscious awareness and forgotten that it has forgotten what has happened, the body has not and never will.

Clearly these emotions have not been dealt with and reacting to them is not dealing with them. To repress or to react to them are two sides of the same coin.

Although the mind uses these defence mechanisms to gain a sense of control, this behaviour only leads the opposite happening. By running away from these emotions, one ultimately ends up enslaved to them. During the time of the traumatic occurrence, it may have enabled one to survive, but as time passes it will only create problems.

Awareness

These two options (reaction or repression) will not lead to any kind of growth or awareness. The emotions have become trapped due to the mind's avoidance, and need to be faced and released.

This doesn't mean endlessly going over these feelings or becoming consumed by them. It means facing them with awareness. If this is done properly, they will be released.

Chapter 44

Rejection

There are many fears that human beings can feel and some of these are classed as real and part of the ability to survive, while others are seen as self-made and have very little to do with survival.

The fear of rejection is often classed as a fear that is irrational and not based in reality. In most cases as an adult, it is unlikely that anything too harmful is going to happen if one is rejected. One's life is not likely to come to an end and one will live for another day.

But while this is often the case and nothing too harmful does take place, it is often irrelevant. This fear can cause so many problems in one's life that it can stop them from going towards what they truly want and need, and cause them to stay where they are in life.

For these people, it is not a fear that is slightly distressing or that has little impact on their life; it is something that is overwhelming. Their life is then defined and ruled by this the fear of rejection.

Frustration

On the surface this is going to have the potential to cause mild to extreme frustration, anger, and hopelessness. There will be some things in one's life that will be put off for a short time and there will be others that are forever put off.

Progress is then something that either happens on the odd occasion or simply never happens. And one then ends up being stuck at a certain level of growth and development. To miss out on certain opportunities and chances could become the norm.

This could relate to some areas of one's life or cover just about every area. One is therefore unlikely to feel too empowered or connected to life and the world around them.

To see other people go after what they want and get it might be a common occurrence, further enhancing their sense of despair and the sense that they have no control over what they do or don't do.

Interpretation

Perhaps one thinks that they haven't got what it takes to go after what they want and that other people have something they lack, for instance. There could be people who tell them to move beyond their fear of rejection and while that sounds easy enough at an intellectual level, it is something that can be far from easy at an emotional level.

This could be a fear that is simply dismissed as just a feeling: that there is nothing more to it. And while it is intended to make one feel better and move beyond this fear, it can just result in the individual feeling weak and that they lack something.

Genders

When it comes to women, this fear might be more acceptable than for men. For women it could be seen as understandable and therefore allow them to be given some kind of support or encouragement.

But for men it could be seen as a sign of weakness, suggesting that the man lacks courage. So a woman could end up feeling that this is normal, and a man could see it as something to be ashamed of.

Different Areas

And this is going to be something that can affect every area of one's life. If this doesn't relate to all areas and only relates to one, it might not be as bad. And yet at the same time, this one area could impact every other. So it won't necessarily matter how pervasive this is; what matters is how strong the fear of rejection is.

The key area is going to be relationships. And this relates to one's career, friends, and relationships with the opposite sex. To move up in one's career or to ask for some kind of pay rise might be sabotaged through one fearing rejection.

And the same can apply to one asking for what they want and need in a relationship and speaking their truth. Perhaps one sees an attractive person that they want to talk to or who they know and would like to take things further.

But in each in each of these situations, fear of rejection takes over and nothing ever happens.

A Closer Look

For the individual that has a fear of rejection that is overwhelming and out of balance, it is highly likely that it is more than just a feeling that they are experiencing: it could be a whole body experience and something that consumes them.

When the feeling of rejection is being experienced or about to be experienced, there is going to be something more to it. Rejection is on the surface and is just one level; what is deeper than the fear of rejection is what it will mean to this person to be rejected.

Emotional Age

Although one is physically an adult, it doesn't mean that they feel like one emotionally. And this is due to someone being emotionally stuck at a certain age or time in their life. So, to look at rejection through the eyes of an adult, it becomes clear that generally nothing too troubling is going to happen.

And yet if one were to look at rejection through the eyes of a child, it is evident that rejection is a matter of life or death. To not receive the right nurturance and attention from one's caregiver, could have resulted in an experience or many experiences that were traumatic.

If these feelings were allowed to be released through their caregivers being emotionally available, it wouldn't be a problem. However, if they are not dealt with, they could have stayed in one's body.

So although one physically grows, emotionally they can still feel like they did all those years ago. And whenever one is in a situation where they want something from another, these trapped feelings and emotions will rise up once again. It doesn't matter then what the other person does or doesn't do, as these feelings are inside one's body and will therefore be triggered in one way or another.

Awareness

To look at this logically, it is obvious that one is overreacting, and yet if they are still carrying all this emotional pain from the past, how else would they feel? To engage in self-blame or to see oneself as lacking something is not helpful and it is not accurate either.

One is simply acting in ways that are a consequence of what has built up within them and of what needs to be released from their body.

Chapter 45

Regression

If defence mechanisms are mentioned, it is likely that regression will be spoken about and this is because it is one of the more common mechanisms. But no matter what defence mechanism is used, they each have the same purpose, with the purpose being that they allow one's mind to avoid the emotional pain of the body.

Although defence mechanisms could be seen as bad things, without them one wouldn't last very long. They allow one to keep pain under control and to regulate what happens to them. Without them one would end up being overwhelmed by pain and life would be unbearable.

However, one can have a tendency to use one defence mechanism more that they use another or even have a few that they use as a way of life. And the reason that they have become accustomed to using a certain one can depend on numerous factors.

Their childhood will play a big role, as will the people that they spend time with and the society that they live in. So the ones they use will typically be what one feels safe with and to use others would be associated as not being safe.

The Build Up

So even though one will need to use these from time to time and could have certain ones operating in their life constantly, the more pain that has built up within them, the more defences they will need to have.

If these defence mechanisms were removed even momentarily, all kinds of pain could arise and this might be too much for someone to cope with - at least if they didn't have the right support around them. One may need to undergo a number of sessions with a therapist or healer.

But with that aside, it is clear that defence mechanisms are similar to the dams that keep water at bay. And just as water would shoot out if the dam wasn't there, emotional pain would appear in the same way if these defences were not in place.

Short Term

One could have a tire that goes flat and as a way to handle this problem, they use the spare. But while this has short-term benefits, it is often not meant to be used constantly. A new tyre will be needed.

And although defence mechanisms do have short-term benefits, when they are used in the long run it can lead to problems. The mind can come to the conclusion that everything is fine and yet the body will still be carrying the emotional pain that appeared through a certain event or a number of events that took place.

Control

These defence mechanisms allow the mind to experience a sense of control. And this is not done through the mind working with one's emotions and being with them, but by trying to control them or through denying their existence.

But although the mind can believe that it is in control by avoiding emotions and therefore the pain that they can create, the whole process can cause one to become more and more out of control.

And yet these defence mechanisms can stop one from realising that this is what is actually happening. What is happening in one's body and what is taking place externally can then seem random and as happening to them, as opposed to being created by them.

As Time Passes

At first, one might be able to deal with this emotional pain without too much trouble, but as time passes and the years go by, it is likely to become out of control. The cracks will start to appear in one way or another.

One could then end up engaging in a lot of projection and what they are not willing to face within themselves, they end up seeing in other people. Here, one can feel that they are being victimised by external factors, but the world is just reflecting back what is going on in their body.

Regression

When it comes to regression, one is returning to a state of being that feels safe. So there will be an external trigger of some kind and based on how one's ego mind interprets this, one will end up feeling a certain way and therefore act in a way that feels comfortable.

This will happen automatically and without one having to think about it. As an adult this is not going to be ideal, as one is likely to regress to a childlike state. So although they are physically an adult, emotionally they will feel like a child - and this is not going to be a child that is happy and full of life.

Childhood

It could be the result of what has happened throughout one's life, but one's childhood years are often the primary cause. So during one's childhood, something would have happened that was traumatic or there could have been an accumulation of minor experiences that were traumatic, causing them to feel certain emotions.

And if these were allowed to be faced and released there wouldn't be a problem. But as they were not released, they will have stayed stuck in one's body. And whenever one is in a situation that reminds them of this early event, they will return to how they felt all those years ago.

The Experience

This could be something subtle and doesn't necessarily need to be something significant. All it could take is: a certain look or vocal tone, a smell, temperature, or word, to find that one has regressed.

They could then end up feeling: hopeless, helpless, vulnerable, ashamed, scared, abandoned, rejected, alone, humiliated, and powerless, amongst other things.

Awareness

So all the time these trapped feelings and emotions are in one's body, it is going to be a challenge for one to be an empowered adult. One might find that they regress during certain moments or that their life is full of these moments and they generally feel out of control and disempowered. These feelings will need to be faced and released.

232

Chapter 46

Regret

When someone takes a certain action or a number of actions that don't lead to the outcome that they desired, there is the chance that they will later come to experience regret. And while there is nothing that one can to do to change what took place, they will suffer nevertheless.

This is likely to include a combination of different thoughts, feelings and sensations. One could ask themselves why they did what they did and/or why they didn't do something else. They could end up feeling angry and this could even develop into rage. And underneath this could the feeling of being powerless or hopeless.

Back And Forth

One minute, one might be feeling down through facing these feelings and the thoughts that are appearing and the next minute, one could be imagining what it would be like if only they had done something different.

In this case, one is likely to feel a sense of relief; if only for a short time. And this is a defence mechanism that the mind will use to regulate how one feels. It won't necessarily change how one feels in the long run, but it will change how they feel in the short term.

Round In Circles

So this could cause one to end up being caught in a cycle. And how long this will last can depend on how willing someone is to face what actually happened. If one is unable to take a step back and see what is taking place, it could be quite some time before they end this cycle.

When someone is down and unable to use their imagination to imagine how it could have been, they are likely to punish themselves. And if one is able to use their imagination, they might feel the urge to do something about what happened.

Guilt

If this relates to something that caused one to feel guilty for instance, it might motivate them to give something back. This could include person that was involved in what later made one feel guilty or it could involve someone else who reminds them of the other person.

So while one might not be able to alter what took place, they are able to change someone else's life in some way. This then gives them a new experience to focus on and this can take away some of the guilt.

A New Experience

Even though what has happened hasn't changed, the new experience can settle the mind down and can give one a reason to feel better and less regretful. The new experience can be used as evidence to prove to oneself that they are not a 'bad person' for example. And how what happened was a once of and doesn't reflect their true nature.

This same experience can also be achieved by one looking back on their life and locating times when they acted in ways that are the complete opposite to what has recently taken place.

Growth

As what has happened has happened and can't be changed, it is clear that one is wasting their energy by punishing themselves. Their energy is being wasted on what has been, instead of being used for what can be.

To reflect on what took place and what one could have done is something that can enhance their life; if this process is used in the right way. When this is done, one will be able to grow and integrate the experience.

Obsession

But if this becomes an obsession and something that one can't stop focusing on, they are going to end up being stuck in the past. In life, sometimes one will do the 'right' thing, and sometimes they won't.

Being human doesn't mean that one has to be perfect; it simply means that one does the best they can. And as everything in life can't be planned; it means that mistakes are going to be made. So instead of punishing oneself for making them, a healthier and more empowering approach would be to see them as being part of life and as examples of what one doesn't want to do in the future.

The Challenge

However, while the ideal is for one to use them as examples of what they don't want to do in life and to move on shortly after, at times one is going to find that they are not able to do this. It is then not that they don't want to move on; it is that they are unable to integrate the experience.

Their mind is going round in circles and like a dog with a bone, it won't let go. Now, one approach would be to say that one needs to 'let go' and to just 'move on', as life is 'too short' to hold onto the past.

And while this can sound logical, and one can't disagree with what is being said, it doesn't mean that one is able to move on.

Trapped Emotions

The mind is generally the point of focus when it comes to change and the body is often ignored. Some people believe that it is ones thoughts that define how they feel and while this can be the case, it can also work the other way around.

How one thinks is then the result of how they feel, and this is why it is not always easy to just 'let go' and 'move on'. Having trapped emotions in one's body will cause the mind to produce certain thoughts. The mind is causing one to have obsessive thoughts as a way to deal with the feelings that are appearing from the body.

Awareness

However, if these feelings were not trapped in one's body, then one wouldn't have the need to have these thoughts in the first place. These trapped emotions will need to be faced and released.

Chapter 47

Relationships

While the ideal might be to have relationships that are always harmonious and are free from pain, during and even when they come to an end, this is not how life works. All relationships have some kind of conflict and if they don't, there is probably a lot of repression taking place.

What will cause some of the conflict will be each person's history, and this will naturally vary. Some people will have a lot of emotional baggage and others won't have quite so much.

Human beings are not meant to be perfect and so having 'issues' is nothing to be ashamed of; it is often more about what one does with what has happened to them, as opposed to what has happened.

Pain

However, although everyone experiences pain in their relationships, not everyone is going to have the same degree of pain. Of course, it is not really possible to directly match one person's experience with another.

The main way to see the difference is how people behave not only in their relationships but also when they experience an end to them.

Emotional Intensity

One way of looking at this pain is to think of it in terms of emotional intensity. If someone is emotionally cut off and numb or out of touch with their emotions for one reason or another, they are unlikely to feel anything.

So with this aside, there is going to be a certain degree of emotional expression taking place for someone who can feel. When one is with another person, it is inevitable that certain emotions will arise. These could be: rejection, abandonment, betrayal, jealousy, anger, powerlessness, guilt, and shame, amongst others.

This emotional experience could also appear when one's relationships come to an end, with it being even stronger than when they were with the other person.

Different Experiences

On one side will be the people who can feel some or even all of the emotions above and more from time to time, and can still be able to maintain a fairly stable relationship. There will be conflict and it won't always be perfect, but there is unlikely to be drama.

And when their relationships end, there are again going to be emotions that are felt. How long the relationships lasted can define how strong one will feel them and yet it could be a shorter one that makes an impact.

Soon after, they will return to feeling emotionally stable, or might even leave before things get too bad. This allows them to avoid a lot of the emotional damage that would have been done if they had held on for longer.

The Other Side

For others, relationships will be highly charged experiences. One could end up feeling every emotion on the spectrum. And while this may mean that they feel good from time to time, it is also going to mean that when they feel 'negative' emotions, they will end up being further down.

This could cause them to come to the conclusion that relationships are not worth the effort and the best thing one could do is to avoid them. The same outlook could also appear when one experiences the end of a relationship.

Loss

It is not something that just causes one to feel a minor sense of loss and sadness for a short time; it could last for many, many months and make them wonder if life is worth living. And if one was with someone for a long time, or if their partner passes on, then this outlook is going to be expected.

When one experiences this as a way of life and/or even when a relationship has not even lasted that long, it is going to cause a lot of suffering in one's life. To have them could be too painful and to avoid them could be no better.

Reasons

Now, through seeing the differences in how people experience pain during their relationships and when they come to an end, it would be normal to come to certain conclusions. One common reason would be to say that some people are simply luckier than others and are very fortunate in life.

One could also say that some people choose the right people and others choose the wrong people. To look at this from a certain perspective would mean that these are valid answers, but while they might sound like they fit, they won't lead to change or allow someone to feel empowered.

Trapped Emotions

One of the reasons why someone can experience the emotional pain that they do in their relationships is because they have trapped emotions in their body. Although these emotions are trapped and one's mind can be cut off from them, they are still having an effect.

They will define who one is attracted to and attracts and they will then cause one to co create situations that will allow them to appear. The challenge is that while they do want to come out and be released, they can just end up making someone feel overwhelmed and victimised.

Patterns

And instead of one seeing that they are a part of what is happening, one can end up believing that other people are making them feel as they do. If one is not aware of what is going on inside, they will not see how what is going on outside is a reflection of their feelings on the inside.

This is why one can end up having relationships with different people and yet have the same emotional experience again and again. These emotions will cause one to create relational patterns that mirror how they feel.

Awareness

One may have trapped emotions due to what has happened in their adult years and these can also go back to childhood. The mind can be cut off from them, but the body doesn't forget.

So in order for one to change how they feel in their relationships and even when they end, they will need to release the trapped emotions from their body.

Chapter 48

Self-control

Control is something that everyone not only wants, but needs to a certain degree. To have no control would make life a real challenge and could make one question their will to live. This does not mean that the control in question here is the control of others.

The type of control this relates to is self-control and having the ability to decide what one will or won't do. To have control over others is one thing, but it is something very different to have it over oneself.

Control is a vital part of life; the defining factor is the kind of control that one is motivated by. If one chooses self-control then they will be seen in one way and if they choose control over others, they will be seen in another way.

Good And Bad

It is the difference between being labelled as a 'good' human being and being labelled a 'bad' human being. And yet beyond these labels is a human being and as human beings we contain these so-called 'good' and 'bad' elements. Some people have realised one and the other remains nothing more than a potential.

Although one person may exercise self-control and the other may try to control others, inherently they are more or less the same. The primary distinction is often due to the kind of people that they have been around from the moment they were born.

Different Degrees

Even though someone is not extremely controlling in their personal or business life, or act as a dictator of a country, for instance, it doesn't mean that they don't need to experience a certain amount of control. The need will be there; it will just be a more balanced need.

It won't be something that has possessed them and ended up taking complete control of their ability to question whether it is right or wrong. What they will do is exercise control in a way that is generally functional and doesn't infringe on the rights of others.

Self-control

This could be the result of them having a healthy level of self-control. Here, one is in control not only of their physical body, but of their mental and emotional sides. And from this inner control, they are able to let go and trust in the process of life without the need to control others.

One is not necessarily always responding to life in this way, as one is only human and there will inevitably be moments when they lose this ability. Being human means that we are not perfect and to aspire to be so would not only be a waste of time, but would be impossible.

So this person could go about getting what they wanted through agreements and mutual consent. Their behaviour would be a choice and seldom reactive. Their words would also be thought-out and carefully chosen.

Control Of Others

When someone has the need to control others and therefore does control them or at least tries to, inner control is not going to be something they are familiar with. This could relate to someone who leads a country, or it could relate to someone who is controlling in all areas of their personal life, or just a certain area.

One may have control of their body, but what they won't necessarily have is emotional control, and their mind is likely to be out of control as a consequence. There is unlikely to be a sense of trust in life or the feeling that life will work out for them without being controlling.

Separation

It could be that they feel separate from life and in order to connect to it, they need to control everything, or just some things. So instead of receiving things through being in resonance with what they seek and realising there is no separation, they try to get things through control as a result of feeling cut off from what they want or need.

How they feel is causing them to see life in a certain way and to experience life as something that is out of their control. Because although one may be seen as someone who likes to control people, at a deeper level they are just trying to control how they feel. And so although people will be involved, they allow one to regulate how they feel.

A Reflection

If one feels completely out of control within, then they will need to exercise more control without. And if it is not this extreme, then the outer control will not be as extreme. The outer will always reflect what is going on within and what makes this difficult to realise is that one cannot directly look inside another human being.

What one can do is observe how they behave and how they don't behave. So the more emotional baggage or weight they are carrying, the more they will need to use control in their life. This will apply to: people, situations, and outcomes. However, the more controlling one is, the more attached they will become, and this very attachment can end up pushing what they seek even further away.

Trapped Emotions

These emotions could have built up since one was a baby and go on to include what has happened in adult life. As a result of them staying trapped in one's body, they have taken over and are defining how one does or does not feel, rather like a parasite that comes in unnoticed. At first, one might sense that something is not right, but as time passes, they can forget how things were and think that how they feel is normal.

Awareness

To have self control one will need to release the emotions and feelings that have built up in their body. It will then be possible for one to gradually settle down within and to find their centre.

Chapter 49

Self-harm

There could be said to be two ways that one can be harmed in this world. One of these is through external means: what others do to them. The other is what one does to oneself. What goes on externally can be noticed and as it is observable to others, others can therefore come to one's assistance and put an end to what is happening.

The same approach is not always possible when it comes to the harm that is committed internally. Other people are not always aware of this form of violence and so it can end up going unnoticed.

However, there are exceptions in both cases. So while external violence is visible and can be observed, it doesn't mean that it is always picked up by people or that anything is done about it.

Just because the violence that is going on within is not as observable, it doesn't mean that other people don't pick up on it, or that there are not clear signs that show someone is harming themselves.

Different Types

This comes down to the fact that there are different types of self-harm, with some of these ways being subtle and some of them being more extreme. As a result of this, self-harm can go on without other people knowing; one can even harm oneself without knowing.

If one is physically harming oneself, other people may become aware of the self-harm. However, one could cover this up through wearing certain types of clothes, or by coming up with different reasons as to why they have a cut or bruise, for instance.

On the other hand, what goes on in a person's mind (in how one talks to oneself, for instance) is not likely to be picked up by other people. What they may do, if they are close enough to this person and have good awareness, is pick it up indirectly through how this person behaves.

A Mystery

So the people that one is close to, such as friends, colleagues, and family, can all be oblivious to what is occurring. One could hide what is going on for them as a way to avoid being labelled in a certain way, and to stop themselves from being rejected, abandoned, or experiencing a heightened level of shame.

But this outlook can simply exist in the mind; certain people around one could end up being supportive, only too happy to do whatever they can to enable one to move on from this challenge.

Other people can then appear to stop one from moving beyond this situation, yet it can be what is going on in one's own mind that is sabotaging the process of reaching out for assistance and support.

Self-harm

While self-harm can range from the subtle to the extreme, there are also many ways in which one can harm oneself. To harm one's physical body in some way is a common example. Some of these ways will be seen as self-harm, but there are others that will not be. These ways are more 'socially accepted' versions and as a result, they can go on without being noticed.

So although one type of harm is being channelled into another type and one is still harming oneself, they can end up feeling more at ease. These types can include: extreme sports, exercise, tattoos, eating, drinking, relationships, and sex, amongst other things.

Conscious And Unconscious

What can define how one harms oneself is how conscious one is of what is going on within them, or whether one is more introverted or extroverted.

One person may just go along with their feelings and thoughts and become consumed by them, whereas another may deny how they feel and end up being drawn to external forms of self harm. In this case, one doesn't physically harm their body themselves; they do it through external means. Here, one has no self-awareness and so pushes their body to do all kinds of things that are potentially dangerous.

A Way Of Life

To have moments where one feels worthless, guilty, or ashamed is relatively normal. But these are just moments and are likely to pass before long. Through feeling this way, one may wonder why they did or didn't do something, and one will go on to have an emotional experience. It is this momentary experience that could cause one to engage in self harm.

However, this will soon pass and one will return to their normal state of being. When it comes to someone who self-harms on a regular basis, they are unable to move on and are emotionally stuck.

Trapped Emotions

This could relate to what one has experienced in their adult years and may go back to what has happened to them as child. And as

249

these feelings and emotions were not dealt with at the time, one will have become emotionally stuck at these moments.

The experiences they have had as an adult or child would have caused them to feel certain emotions and feelings. These could be: anger, hate, rage, worthlessness, emptiness, helplessness, powerless, shame, guilt, and fear.

These feelings then create the need for an emotional release and one will use self-harm as a way to regulate how they feel. What these options will do is last for a short time, but what they won't do is deal with the feelings and emotions on a long-term basis.

So they are short-term solutions at best and this is why one will continually feel the need to harm oneself.

Awareness

When these trapped feelings and emotions are released from one's body, one will have no reason to harm oneself. And this is because one will no longer feel the same and as a result of this, self-harm won't be necessary.

Chapter 50

Sensitive

There are some people who are described as being overly sensitive and highly empathic. And while this does lead to many benefits, there are also many challenges that arise from being this way. These people can feel like sponges that pick up anything and everything that is going on within an environment.

Others who are sensitive - but perhaps not to the same degree - can find that they take everything to heart. One word, look, or a certain tone of voice can leave them feeling emotionally overwhelmed.

If the world was suited to this kind of person, it would make their lives a lot easier. Yet in a lot of cases, it is more suitable for people who feel numb and cut off from their feelings. Here, one is not in touch with their feelings, let alone being sensitive, and is unable to feel.

Two Extremes

So even though both extremes carry challenges, to feel numb is more suited to the modern-day world. This is not to say that this is an absolute truth and that sensitive people have no place or cannot thrive. What emotional numbness typically relates to is the corporate environment and to areas where people are out of touch with themselves.

In these types of environments, it is not always seen as abnormal to be emotionally cut off from oneself or to find that emotional masks are worn; it is often seen as normal and how life is. Based on this, one could come to the conclusion that being sensitive is a bad thing and something that needs to be changed in some way.

Two Types Of Criticism

This could lead to some kind of self-harm and one could feel a sense of shame for being this way. As they don't match up to what most people are like, they could come to conclude that it would be easier to be like other people who are not sensitive. And while being like people who are not as sensitive might be easier in some instances, there are many benefits that one would lose.

To be critical of oneself is one thing, yet it is another thing to receive criticism from others. One could receive all kinds of labels from others and if they are not sensitive themselves, this would be easy as they are unaware of what it is like to be sensitive.

If one has not experienced something or one is not very empathic oneself, it can be difficult to really understand what another is experiencing. Some of the things others could say are that: one is too sensitive; what they said was only a joke; they need to grow up; they shouldn't take things so personally; that they should just let it go, and they shouldn't get so worked up.

Logic

Now, these viewpoints that come from another's mouth can sound logical and one might even agree with them, but that is about as far as it goes. If things were as easy as simply internalising these views and becoming less sensitive, one would surely do just that.

However, it is not as simple as this and so no matter what another person's mind comes up with or what one thinks themselves, it is not necessarily going to make any difference.

The Other Option

There are some people who are sensitive at one point and gradually end up becoming insensitive. This can cause them to be critical of people who are sensitive, as these people could remind them of what they have denied within themselves.

Perhaps they resorted to alcohol, food, drugs, or some kind of muscle-building to tone down their sensitive side, and so went from being overly sensitive to feeling very little in the majority of cases.

One could also go from one extreme to the other, sometimes feeling numb and at other times feeling extremely sensitive. This could depend on what is going on in this person's life, for example.

Examples

For people who are overly sensitive, the feeling could impact every area of their life or could just include certain areas. One may not be able to handle any kind of feedback from others, whether negative or constructive, despite being offered with the best of intentions.

Relationship break-ups could be another area that wipes a person out, leaving them completely overwhelmed. To be in places full of people, loud noises, or big crowds may be another hot point. People who are loud, forceful, or controlling could also cause problems.

One might do their best to avoid all conflict or confrontation and have difficulty standing up for themselves. Or, to watch the news or to be in situations where people are suffering might be too much to handle.

Reasons

Now, there are going to be numerous reasons why someone is overly sensitive. For starters, their nervous system is different to someone who experiences life differently. One thing that can cause someone to have no control over their arousal level is when they have trapped emotions and feelings.

As they are trapped in one's body, it can affect one's nervous system and cause one to have a heightened level of arousal, either at certain times or as a way of life. These could be from one's adult years but could go right back to when one was a child or a baby.

So this could be due to an event that was extremely traumatic or to an accumulation of minor events that caused pain, for instance. And as these have remained in one's body, one has very little choice in how they feel; it is then an involuntary reaction and not a conscious choice.

Awareness

This is not to say that one will lose their ability to be sensitive by releasing these trapped emotions and feelings. But it could mean that their arousal level will settle down and that their nervous system will mirror this change. So although one will still be sensitive, they may no longer be overly sensitive. It could also result in one forming better boundaries to protect their sensitive nature.

Chapter 51

Shame

To be human means that we are emotional beings and there are many emotions that we can have. Shame is one of them and this can stop one from acting in ways that are inappropriate, for example. And yet this emotion can also end up taking over one's life. It is then no longer something that is aiding one's life; it is something that is controlling their entire existence.

This is why shame is often divided into two categories and these are described as: healthy and unhealthy. So when it comes to healthy shame, one may end up feeling shame if they were to go shopping without wearing any clothes.

When it comes to unhealthy shame, a person may go out shopping with clothes on and still feel shame. For this person it doesn't matter what they wear or what they do, the feeling is still there.

The feeling could be something that is always there, or it could come and go at certain times and all depend on what one is doing. Healthy shame, on the other hand, is there to stop one from acting in ways that are not in one's best interests.

Personal And Impersonal

Healthy shame is not something that is personal; it is impersonal and based on what one does. So although one might feel bad after doing something, it won't be taken to heart and internalised: it will be a feeling that soon passes.

However, unhealthy shame will be taken personally and will not simply be something one does, but who they are. It is something that has become one's identity and doesn't disappear after a certain period of time. And no matter how much times passes, the feeling is still there.

Here, one can come to the conclusion that there is something inherently wrong with them and they are completely flawed. There is then very little, if anything, that one thinks they can do to change.

Consequences

To have this deep sense that one is flawed and different to others has the potential to create all kinds of unpleasant consequences. But just because one feels this way, it doesn't mean that it will always be noticeable.

It is possible for someone to come across in a way that gives off the impression that they lack belief in themselves and yet it is also possible that someone will behave in a way that causes one to see them as being full of belief and confidence.

Here, one is either getting caught in feelings of shame or they are avoiding them by creating adaptive behaviours and ways of handling life that are the complete opposite.

Abuse

When one feels a sense of shame they can also end up passing it onto other people. This is typically something that will go on unconsciously and won't be something that one is aware of doing. Ultimately, they will do this to regulate how they feel and to give them a short-term release from the pain that they are experiencing.

This shame can then be passed onto whoever one spends their time with. So if one has children, it could end up being passed on to them.

If one is a teacher, it could end up being passed on to pupils. One's friends or colleagues could also pick it up through being around them in ways that are either obvious or subtle.

There will be some people who hold their shame in and don't pass it onto others. However, one might hold it in during certain moments and express it in others. One person won't necessarily be one way or the other; they could be both.

The Mind

Along with these feelings of shame are going to be certain thoughts and beliefs that one has. These thoughts could be that: one is useless; one is worthless; one does not deserve to exist; one is inferior; one is invisible; there is something inherently wrong with them; and others look down on them.

It is common for these thoughts to be labelled as the reason why one feels as they do, and that one's thoughts create their feelings and emotions. As a result of this outlook, one could change their thoughts and beliefs into something more empowering.

And for some people this will work, but for others it won't be enough. The reason for this is that these thoughts are often nothing more than a reflection of what is going on in one's body. It is then not so much that one's thoughts are creating their feelings, as it is that their feelings are creating their thoughts.

The Body

What is going on in the body is often ignored and the mind ends up getting all of the attention. Yet this can be a real mistake, causing one to look for answers in the wrong place. One can then not only end up feeling frustrated and powerless due to nothing changing, but they can also waste a lot of time.

These feelings of shame that reside in the body could be there due to what happened in one's adult years and may also be the result of what took place when they were a child. As one didn't get the chance to release these feelings, they will have stayed trapped in one's body and primarily above their stomach.

Possible Reasons

There are also likely to be other feelings along with shame that have remained trapped in the body. The reason they have stayed in the body could be due to a number of reasons.

Perhaps one was brought up by a caregiver who was verbally abusive and so they ended up feeling shame and had no other choice but to hold it in. Perhaps one's caregivers may have become unaware themselves, and ended up passing the trait on through what they didn't do, as much as what they did do.

Awareness

So while one could deal with their thoughts, the feelings would still remain in their body. It might be better to release these trapped feelings and emotions and then their thoughts will naturally change.

Chapter 52

Suicidal

There are many challenges in today's world and the area of suicide is one of those. This can relate to people who are committing suicide or to people who feel suicidal and who would like to end their life in some way.

Mental and emotional problems have become the norm in the western world. But even though this is a serious problem, it not something that is openly spoken about in most cases. And just like depression or any other kind of internal challenge that one can have, it is has become a taboo.

So although someone can be crying out for assistance and for solutions to their internal challenges, there is an invisible barrier that can stop one from reaching out for the support one desperately needs.

Exposure

In order for one to be assisted with their mental or emotional problems, one will need to feel that it safe to do so. And when other people, such as celebrities or influential people, stand up and express what they are going through or have gone through, it can remove a lot of these invisible barriers.

Here, one can start to see that how they think or feel is actually normal, and that these feelings are not something that one needs to feel ashamed of and do not mean that something is inherently wrong with them. As awareness increases, it can remove one's sense of isolation and the feeling that one is the only person who has a certain challenge.

This is why awareness is so important; while something is hidden and not spoken about, it can result in one suffering in silence. One may be surrounded by people or spend a lot of time by themselves, but if one feels that they have to hide what they are going through, it won't matter whether one is alone or has people around them.

The Ideal

In an ideal world, mental and emotional problems wouldn't exist. But without going that far, the ideal would be for them to be accepted and seen for what they are: a sign that something is not right within and needs to be looked at with compassion, care, and acceptance.

These problems should not be judged as: bad, wrong, or shameful. When something is resisted it often leads to its continuation and when something is faced and embraced, it can often lead to some kind of resolution.

Avoidance

While facing something can put an end to the effects it is having, avoiding something can cause these effects to become more powerful. This relates to all areas of life, from weeds in a garden to relational conflicts. If these issues are faced, it can minimise the challenges that have appeared, while if they are ignored, they can become completely out of control.

So instead of one having a healthy sense of control, one can end up being controlled by these occurrences. Emotions and feelings are no different here; if they are avoided and not released in some way, they can completely take over.

Emotional Build-up

If one didn't form a healthy relationship with their emotions and feelings as a child, it is unlikely that one is going to form a new relationship with them as they get older. Perhaps one could seek out assistance and take personal responsibility, but this is often the exception as opposed to the rule.

When it comes to the education system or the healthcare system, one is unlikely to learn about emotions and feelings. These are generally ignored and are seen as insignificant. What society does is provide a way to avoid emotions and feelings.

So one can avoid them and cover them up, but they don't simply disappear; they build up in the body. And as they build, they have more power and influence over what one does and, more importantly, over how one feels.

Being Overwhelmed

It doesn't take much reflection to realise that this is going to lead to certain consequences taking place. And what may have started out as a feeling that was fairly moderate and not too overwhelming can easily come to cause one to feel completely overpowered and trapped.

One needs to go into water to physically experience drowning, but one can also feel that they are drowning in their feelings and emotions. These can range from a feeling or combination of feelings that are simply overwhelming, leaving one with the feeling that everything has become out of their control and is now too much to handle.

The Occurrence

For some people, this will be an experience they have had their whole life and it could then seem normal and how life is. For others, this can have appeared as a result of some kind of loss: either the loss of a job, of a loved one, or of a relationship that has come to an end.

One of the biggest factors in whether one has felt this way their whole life or whether the feeling has appeared during one's adult years is in how one's emotions were responded to as a child.

Childhood

As a child, one doesn't have the ability to emotionally regulate themselves. The brain is not developed enough to deal with emotions and so it is vital that one has a caregiver that can assist in this process.

When one experienced emotions as a child, it can feel like the end of the world and one can easily become overwhelmed by them. If one had a caregiver that was emotionally available, this is not going to be a problem. Through having a caregiver like this, one's emotions, in the majority of cases, will be regulated. Here, one will be able to develop their own ability to regulate their emotions, learning that it is safe to seek support in others when supporting oneself is not possible.

Unavailable Caregiver

If one was brought up by a caregiver that was emotionally unavailable and out of tune with their needs, then this important process is unlikely to take place. As a child experiencing emotional unrest and unease, one will have had to simply sit in their emotions and feelings as there was no one around to show them how to regulate their emotions.

As one does not have the ability to do this at such a young age, it can result in all kinds of problems. The feeling of wanting to die and of wanting one's life to end is going to be normal. These feelings are far too much for one to cope with as a child, but as no one is there, one has very little choice in the matter.

Consequences

These emotions and feelings will have to be pushed into one's body. Not only is there an emotional build-up occurring, but one didn't learn how to regulate their emotions either. This is then like having a challenge and yet having no idea how to overcome it.

The original experience of becoming overwhelmed by emotions can then stay with someone for their whole life, or perhaps an occurrence in later life may retrigger these early experiences.

Awareness

One can feel overwhelmed and trapped on the inside, and society can then further this experience as a result of overlooking emotions. If many people have had a childhood like this and do all they can to avoid their emotions, it is not surprising that society is so emotionally unaware.

Society is then mirroring what is going on for the majority of people. Emotions and feelings are neither good nor bad, but have become such a challenge due to them having built up, becoming out of control.

Chapter 53

Ungrounded

This is a term that is typically heard in the area of spirituality and self-development, and describes a state where someone can feel a bit spaced out and disconnected from the earth. Perhaps one has engaged in some kind of energy healing or spiritual practice. It can even take place when one has been reading for a while or has used a computer for a certain amount of time.

Another description that can relate to someone who feels ungrounded is dissociation. Here, one feels that they are not connected to their body, let alone the earth. And this can be a relatively new experience and therefore noticeable, or can be the only thing one has known, meaning they may not even realise it.

Taking these different examples into account, it shows that one can feel ungrounded during certain moments of their life or as an entire way of life. And modern day technology can play a part in this, as well as spiritual practices that have been around for years.

Momentary Problem

If one is around computers and technology a lot or has a job that is highly focused on using their mind for instance, this is likely to be something that comes and goes. At the time one may or may not be aware of what is taking place, due to how focused one is upon the task at hand. And yet when one gets up to go for a walk or has a break, it will often become clear that they are not in their body.

Before long, this experience will generally have passed and one will return to feeling like a whole human being. This person will know what has taken place and will have experienced it many times before, and so there won't be the need to do anything else.

If this disconnection lasts longer that it normally does or doesn't go away even after one has stopped what they are doing, it would be necessary to start asking questions.

A Way Of Life

When it comes to feeling ungrounded during each and every day of one's life, then clearly something is not right. Computers could be used in one's career or as a part of one's life in general; however, one may not even notice that they are in their head, as this may be what it is always like for them. So no matter if one uses computers or not, one's experience of life is the same.

If one has recently had an experience that pushed them out of their body and caused them to be dissociated, then they might notice what is taking place. This could take a while to realise, though, as what happened could be so traumatic that one no longer remembers how things used to be.

Normal

To go even further than this would be the individual that has always experienced life more or less in this way, and who therefore doesn't think about there being any other way. It is like a fish in water: that experience of life is the only one that is known. As the saying goes: 'we don't know what we don't know'.

Consequences

To feel ungrounded on the odd occasion is unlikely to create too many problems. It could be said that feeling ungrounded is a by-product of living in the modern-day world, with its reliance on technology. And as nature plays a much smaller role in modern-day societies, which are filled with concrete, it can be harder to connect with the earth.

So to live in one's head and cut off from one's body is going to occur from time to time, but generally one will soon be back in their body. However, when this is a way of life and one is always in their head, the consequences can be severe.

Ungrounded

There are going to be extremes here and some will be more manageable than others. For some people this could lead to memory loss, not knowing what they did a few moments ago. The mind can create a lot of mental energy and so to be stuck in there can cause one to feel restless, have a short attention span, and even be labelled as having attention deficit disorder.

To feel disconnected from the rest of existence can be normal and this will include: people, nature, animals, and one's body. It could be a mystery as to what one is feeling and what one's needs and wants are. Anxiety could also be an emotion that one is familiar with and experience on a regular basis. Having intimate relationships with others may also be a challenge and all because one is disconnected from their feelings and emotions.

The mind could turn this experience into a story and cause one to feel as though they are from another planet or they could have visions of leaving their body. There are many other possible consequences.

Solutions

For some people, taking a break from what makes them feel ungrounded and spending time in nature may be enough. However, if someone always feels disconnected from their body and the earth, then that is not going to be enough. To feel ungrounded during certain moments is one thing and it something very different to feel ungrounded most of the time.

Trapped Emotions

When something is painful, it is natural for one to leave their body and go into their head. This is an act of survival and is not wrong or bad. Trauma is typically described as an experience where one feels powerless and this means that one won't feel safe enough to go through their feeling cycle. If they could feel what took place, it would allow them to process what happened and move on.

And trauma is not always a big event either; it could be an accumulation of lots of little things that gradually wear someone down. So when one doesn't feel safe enough to feel their feelings, it is then normal for one to move their awareness into their head. The body becomes an area of pain and something that one will do their best to avoid. So these trapped feelings and emotions cause one to leave their body, and while they are there, one is unlikely to return into their body.

Awareness

So as one releases their trapped feelings and emotions they may find that they return to living in their body and only live in their head when it is appropriate. This might be something they have never experienced before or something they are used to experiencing.

Chapter 54

Victim Mentality

There is nothing like a good victim story to get people's attention. The media routinely covers a certain event or situation where one person or a group of people are labelled as victims. Based on what happens in these situations, it is often very difficult to disagree with this description.

Sometimes these stories relate to what the average guy on the street has done and at other times, they can cover what a person of authority has done: for example, governmental figures, people of wealth and status, and other socially elevated individuals.

At a personal level, this can include: what friends have or haven't done, what one's lover has or hasn't done, and what one's family has or hasn't done. This can also include colleagues and managers.

Meaning

The meaning of a victim on Google is described as –
1. A person harmed, injured, or killed as a result of a crime, accident, or other event or action.
2. A person who is tricked or duped: "the victim of a hoax".

And so if one has a victim mentality they constantly feel harmed and injured. It is then not an experience that they have from time to time, but a state of mind.

An Identity

To feel like a victim from time to time is probably fairly normal. Things happen and so one will not always get what they want or have things go to plan, which may leave one feeling slightly or even extremely victimised.

But this will be an experience that soon passes in most cases. However, there are other people who do not have this experience on the odd occasion, but on a regular basis. It has become as familiar as breathing to them.

A General Outlook

So although this could relate to just one area of life, it can go on to be a factor in all areas of one's life. Here, one could feel victimised: by society, in one's relationships, in one's workplace, and even by healthcare professionals.

One may also just have one area of life where they continually feel hard done-by and downtrodden. Because this is how they feel on the inside, they will always be drawn to external examples of people who are in the same position.

Validation

This will give them a sense of validation and acknowledgment. One will be able to feel that they are not alone in their pain and struggle, and that other people are going through the same thing. It may also give one a sense of relief to see other people suffering and to see that they are not the only one.

In the same way, when certain authority figures or people in power end up being victimised, this might make one feel a sense of revenge and the feeling that some form of payback has taken place.

This is why victim stories in the media are so popular and is why they receive so much exposure; they mirror how so many people feel in the world.

Emotional Experience

There are going to be two levels to this experience. One side may be to feel anger, and other expressions of anger can then occur. These can be: hate, revenge, resentment, and rage. These are clear signs that some kind of compromise has taken place.

Through feeling this way, one is able to avoid what is going on at a deeper level. Anger is often used as a form of protection and as an alert that one is being taken advantage of.

Underneath the anger and its other forms will be a sense of powerlessness and a lack of control. One may feel that they have been violated.

The Observer

Someone with a victim mentality may feel that this is how life is and that they have no control over what is taking place. The mind can make one believe that they are just observing these situations and that this is all happening randomly.

But the real answers as to why one keeps finding oneself in these situations will be found in the body. At a deeper level, this is what the ego mind has come to associate as familiar and therefore safe. And so even though this is causing one to experience endless suffering and pain, it is what the ego feels comfortable with.

Causes

There could have been a time in one's later life when one felt victimised, but it is usually due to what happened as a child. It is these early moments that will often define whether one feels like a victim or not.

The ideal is to have a caregiver that is empathic and emotionally available. Here one's needs and wants will generally be met, and one's emotions and feelings will be acknowledged and regulated in most cases.

But in some cases this doesn't happen and this can be due to having a caregiver that is unempathic, emotionally unavailable, and out of tune, causing the child or baby's needs and wants will be ignored in most cases. During times of emotional unrest and unease, one may be left to become overwhelmed by their emotions.

Consequences

These are general guidelines of course, but they are a rough idea of what can happen. So if one has had an unempathic caregiver, there is a higher chance that one will end up feeling that they have no control and are powerless; to feel like a victim would be a natural consequence.

Because if a caregiver is out of touch with their own needs and emotions it will be normal for them to ignore and deny their child's needs and wants. The child could then end up being used to fulfil their needs and wants.

On one side of the spectrum this could be fairly harmless and not lead to too many challenges, but on the other it could involve mild to extreme abuse. If this takes place, it is only natural that one will come to see themselves as a victim, because the person or persons meant to care for and protect them ended up taking advantage of them.

Reality

The feelings and emotions that one experienced during these times of being taken advantage of would then have been pushed outside of one's awareness. While one may have felt this way towards a caregiver, one still needed them to survive: so their existence had to be denied.

One's ego mind would have come to associate these experiences as being familiar and therefore safe.

So even though they were painful or even traumatic, they came to be known as normal and as what to expect from others. This means that one would continually end up in situations that validate these early experiences, because this is what feels comfortable at a deeper level.

Awareness

It would be easy to say that people with a victim mentality need to think positively or change how they think. But while this approach deals with the mind, it doesn't deal with what's taking place in the body.

The feelings that have remained in the body since those early moments will have to be released. One needs to grieve what happened and then it will go. And as these feelings are released, one's tendency to feel like a victim will start to alleviate and as this happens one's reality will change.

Chapter 54

Releasing Your Trapped Emotions

When it comes to releasing the trapped emotions from your body, it might be necessary for you to seek some kind of external support. I say this because when these feelings have built up for so long, they can end up being overwhelming once they are brought to the surface.

They might already be at the surface, and so feeling overwhelmed could be something you are already familiar with. But if you are not in touch with your trapped emotions already, it might be a challenge for you to get in touch with them.

Patterns

You might be aware of certain patterns in your life and yet be completely out of touch with the trapped emotions that are causing these patterns to continually appear.

Not only will the external support allow you to get in touch with your trapped emotions, it will also allow you to release them more easily. Through this support, they are holding the space and assisting you in going somewhere you might not go by yourself.

Reaching out for assistance is not something to feel bad about; it is something that takes courage. No one is their own island and we all need the support of others.

Feeling Safe

An important part of releasing trapped emotions is feeling safe, and when this is not the case, it can be harder to let go. So whether you are by yourself or in the presence of another person, it is vital that you feel safe enough to let go.

If you are in the presence of another and you don't feel safe, there is a strong chance that this will sabotage the process. It is therefore important to listen to your inner guidance and to work with someone you can trust.

And it may take a while for this trust to form, but the main thing is that you see that it can form.

Healing Options

Now, we are all different and what works for one person might not work for another; the technique or therapy involved is often secondary to what the healer or therapist is like. This comes down to the fact that you need to feel safe and believe that they can assist you.

If you don't believe the other person can assist you or you don't feel safe, it won't matter what they do. Finding a therapist that will assist you in facing your emotions and then releasing them is one option.

Something that I have found useful is SHEN therapy. This is a hands-on technique that will enable you to get in touch with your emotions and gradually release them.

I have also experienced Tantric massage, and this allowed me to let go and to be affirmed.

There are many other options out there and just because something works for one person, it doesn't mean that it will work for another. This is why I can't suggest one technique or healing method as being the only answer.

Mirroring

Not only will you release your trapped emotions through the assistance of another, you will also be mirrored and affirmed by them. And if the reason you have trapped emotions is because you were neglected growing up, they will supply what you didn't get all those years ago.

The attunement that the therapist or healer will provide can be just as important as it is for you to release your trapped emotions.

Grieving

This is going to be time where you will be grieving your unmet childhood needs. Through crying out the pain of not getting your developmental needs met, you will gradually be able to let go of the emotional build-up within you.

The external support of another person or a support group may be needed in the beginning, but as time passes, this may be something you can do by yourself. There may be times when you wonder if anything is happening, and this is because it is not a linear process.

Another Approach

If you have been releasing your emotions for a while and your life doesn't change, it may mean that you need to try another approach. This is because we can carry the pain of our ancestors, and even though this is causing us to sabotage our life, we hold on through the need to be loyal.

As a result of this, we can suffer like our ancestors did, and we do this out of love. So just like there can be patterns in our own life, there can also be generational patterns.

If this is something you can relate to, you can work with someone who uses family constellations. This is something that can take place in a one-to-one session or in a workshop.

Persistence

What matters is that you keep going and don't give up. While this process is not easy, it is what will allow you to be emotionally free.

My Story

When I first got into personal development, I wanted to experience more confidence. But as time went on and I came to understand myself more, I started to see that what I really wanted to experience was more emotional control. At this time, my emotions were completely out of control and I felt powerless to do anything about them.

To use a metaphor: I was like a small boat on the ocean, being tossed around and having very little choice in what took place. The ideal would have been for me to be more like a cruise ship, as to be on this kind of ship would mean that while the water was still around, it would offer a completely different experience.

At the time, I didn't know that my life could be any different; I didn't really know much about emotions either. This was in two thousand and three. But even though this was the year that I decided to do something about my challenges, my emotions had been causing me problems for as long as I could remember.

It took me another ten years of more or less constant study, to find a way to deal with my emotions. Around this time, I also began to truly understand why I had emotional problems in the first place.

The Trigger

While my emotions had always caused me problems, the end of a relationship made things even worse. It was as if these emotions had been in the background of my life, coming to the surface on the odd occasion, but now they were in the foreground.

I was overwhelmed by them. If I had had no awareness of how I had felt for most of my life, I would have said that these had come out of nowhere. However, in reality, the emotions I was experiencing had always been around.

Back In Time

Through reading books about childhood development, and becoming aware of my feelings and the images associated with them, I started to get an idea of what happened to me during my childhood.

I came to realise that I was neglected for long periods of time as a baby and that no one was around to look after me, and this caused a lot of pain. My mind had come to forget what happened, but my body continued to carry the emotional pain of what took place.

Neglect

At this age, being left alone is overwhelming. So not only did I want to die and feel as though I was going to die, I also felt many other emotions. These were: anger, rage, powerlessness, hopelessness, grief, abandonment, rejection, and fear.

Through being left for such long periods of time, being alone is what started to feel safe. So when attention did come, it caused me to feel: fearful, overwhelmed, trapped, smothered, and powerless.

So as my mother was emotionally unavailable and did have the ability to read emotions, I was neglected. It was then inevitable that when she did give me attention it was out of sync with my true needs and wants, simply because the attunement wasn't there, and this is why I ended up feeling smothered by the attention she did give me.

Growing Up

My life then carried on and nothing was done to deal with this early pain. I just thought that something was wrong with me and that there wasn't a reason for it. Through not having someone there to regulate my emotions, I grew up without this ability. My emotional age didn't really change either.

And while I wasn't completely aware of these emotions that had remained in my body, my life was still being defined by them. My behaviour and the circumstances I found myself in were often a reflection of these trapped emotions, as were the people I was attracted to and attracted into my life.

I felt depressed at times and as though I wanted my life to end. Feeling a sense of personal power was something I rarely, if ever, experienced.

Intimacy

If people got too close to me I would often feel just as I did as a baby; it was too much. And yet if people were not there, I would often feel abandoned. So this created extreme conflict, and whatever happened, I would still suffer. Although experiencing intimacy was something I needed, I didn't feel safe with it.

I felt safe around friends, for instance, and had women in my life on the odd occasion, but that was as far as it got. For years I didn't know why this was, and I ended up feeling like a victim and creating all kinds of other stories about why my life was the way it was.

Healing

For around seven years, I tried different healing techniques, went on courses, and worked with different people, but it was only after all this time that I was ready to face my emotions. And this is when I came to realise that I had trapped emotions in my body that needed to be released.

Validation

Even though I had come to understand what had happened through reading and self-awareness, I hadn't had a family member validate what had happened to me as a baby. So while I was pretty sure, there was still doubt in my mind.

This all changed when I met someone who looked after me as a baby and for a few years afterwards. They were unsure about telling me, but what I was told validated what I had come to realise myself. I then came to see that how I had felt for so long was normal based on what took place, and that there was a reason.

Acknowledgments

I am extremely grateful for all of the help and support that I have had in the past few years that have made this book a reality.

And I am truly grateful to the people who were around during this emotionally challenging time in my life. These include: Adam Jordan, Brian Reynolds, Evette Carter, Lewis Keen, Tony Stuart, Sheila Baynham, Thomas Leahy, Sue Cook, Stuart Wiggins, Keith Lawrence, Glenn and Tracy Needham. Some of these people were aware of how much of an impact they were having and some weren't, but they all played a part. The part they played will never be forgotten.

I would also like to thank: Dov Baron, Jonice Webb, Jasmin lee Cori, Susan Foreward, Karyl Mcbride, David Richo, Pia Melody, Tian Dayton and Conrad W Baars.

And thank you to Michelle, for her loving touch and presence. Through meeting her, I was able to receive something for the first time.

I am grateful to Maddie Northern for taking the time to edit this book and to Carmen Hernandez, for her assistance with arranging parts of book.

Since the moment I came in contact with Susan Winter she has offered nothing but support, so thank you.

About The Author

In 2003, Oliver JR Cooper began the journey of learning about who he was and understanding what life was all about. He read vast amounts of psychological books, took courses and actively worked on his own transformational healing.

Keeping a journal to track his process of insight and discovery, Oliver felt compelled to share this information with others who are also seeking an effective means of internal transformation. In four years, Oliver has written over 520 articles that garnered over 250,000 click-throughs so far.

His Topic Genres include: Abuse, Behaviour, Boundaries, Defense Mechanisms, Emotional Intelligence, Happiness, Men's Psychology, Movie Metaphors, Relationships, Self-Image, Self-Realisation, Social Causes, The Ego Mind and Women's Psychology.

Oliver JR Cooper also offers transformational coaching and has recently started a new project called "Communication Made Easy".

To find out more about Oliver, please go to:

www.oliverjrcooper.co.uk

Made in the USA
Charleston, SC
27 January 2016